COP IN THE CLASSROOM

COP IN THE CLASSROOM

LESSONS I'VE LEARNED,
TALES I'VE TOLD

Sgt. Jim Potter

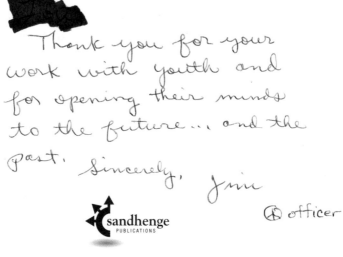

Thank you for your
work with youth and
for opening their minds
to the future... and the
past. Sincerely,
Jim
☮ officer

sandhenge
PUBLICATIONS

Cover design by George Foster

Printed in the United States of America

In the interest of privacy, espec███████entity of
children in this book, names, and occasionally descriptions of individuals have been altered.

The author advises that a few encounters were
disguised because the current officers mentioned
are expert shots and the former students are now
attorneys.

ISBN 0-9790697-7-7
ISBN 978-0-9790697-7-2

Library of Congress Control Number 2007900381

Sandhenge Publications
P.O. Box 1172
Hutchinson, KS 67504-1172
www.copintheclassroom.com

To Alex,
for everything...

Contents

PART II: WHAT ABOUT YOUR JOB?

PART III: WHAT ABOUT THE CHILDREN?

PART IV: WHAT ABOUT THE ADULTS?

PREFACE

I've noticed over the years that children have no shortage of questions. Some of the classrooms I visit as a school resource officer promote the use of question boxes, but at no time or place am I exempt from curious inquiries. I've been stopped in the hallway, encouraged by inquisitive kids to sit next to them during lunch, confronted at recess and even questioned during after duty hours when I've been spotted shopping at local businesses, i.e., "Where's your uniform?" Everyone, it seems, especially kids, have questions for me about being a deputy sheriff.

No subject is off limits to what our youth want to know. They want to learn if my gun is loaded, if I've shot anyone, about car chases, arrests, and if I've had to watch anyone die. They want to know when I first started thinking about being an officer, how to become a cop and whether I like my job. Besides wanting to learn about drugs, alcohol and violence, they also want to know, on the lighter side, what's the funniest thing that's happened to me on duty.

This book is a compilation of some of the common and unique questions that I've received in the schools for over twenty years while serving as a sheriff's deputy. In addition, some of the inquiries I address here using stories are from parents, teachers and myself. Each chapter title is in the question form as it was posed to (or by) me. The answers I share are personal essays inspired from my experiences on the job.

From the first question a child ever asked me about my duties as a police officer, I've enjoyed the teaching experience. The queries from young, developing, lively minds stimulate and spark my own curiosity. They teach me that no question is unimportant and that every questioner, usually a child, is always worthy and deserving of my response. I recognize that they are attempting to understand why and how we do what we do.

— ACKNOWLEDGMENTS —

I give credit and thanks to my parents who always encouraged me to have a love of learning. They also knew the value of a formal education and supported me in that endeavor.

My parents grew up during the Great Depression. Both of them and their families understood sacrifice and success. Due to economic conditions, my mother, though the valedictorian in her class, was unable to attend college. My father, who also excelled in high school, usually had more dirt in his pockets than money, but found a way to graduate from junior college. This was prior to World War II becoming a priority for him and our country. After he was demobilized, his efforts shifted. Even though he was working full time, because of the G.I. bill, he was able to become a university graduate.

The reason this story of education is so important to me is that my parents recognized its importance to them. Mom had to go to work and Dad had to go to war. Later, as I was growing up, it was understood that one of their goals was to give their children the opportunity, if we wished, to earn a college education. It was something they didn't want us to miss.

What I didn't know about my dad, as I struggled in high school, was that his father had not supported his academic efforts. In fact, Grandpa thought school was a waste of time and money! I can only imagine the stressful encounters between father and son.

By my father making an empowering decision to do something that his family had not done before—attend college—he became a trailblazer, affecting future generations in our family, giving me greater exposure to the academic and abstract world of words.

When I attended Lesley College (now a university) my thesis was on school resource officers in Kansas. Even as I was writing that scholarly paper, using qualitative research interviews, I was thinking about *Cop in the Classroom.* For the university thesis I developed themes from other school resource officers, then examined how they related to a peaceable school culture. For this future book I wanted to examine themes established by my students. Their curiosities and concerns, often in question form, became my focus and eventually the title of many of the personal essays.

Writing for me became fluid and fun when I wrote a short story entitled, "Hubcap Houdini." This fictional account of our actual companion rooster (who woke me up well before dawn everyday), marked my resurgence to writing. After its completion, I was encouraged with specific, positive feedback from friends Jean and Russ, Joelle, Carol and Letty.

Then I wrote a play, "Under the Radar: Race at School," that would have never been award-winning without the encouragement of my wife, Alex, to enter it in a statewide competition. The Kansas Arts Council formally agreed with her assessment as they publicly acknowledged my creative work, already being used in diversity workshops.

The reason I mention former projects and their supporters in acknowledgments here is that this book has been a quiet, below the radar, maturing labor of love for several years. Thus, there are few people to thank! I am grateful to our two cats, Gray and Homes, for assisting Hubcap in awakening me early every morning. While I suspect their motives were selfish, I acknowledge their influence on my writing schedule, comparable to middle of the night newspaper carriers.

Besides Alex, the people that made this book possible were unaware of my intentions: administrators at our Sheriff's Department for my assignment in the schools, the trust of educators throughout our county, and of course, the children and youth for their continued friendship, questions and stories. These young people, after all my years as a school resource officer, continue to amaze and delight me. Many of them, despite our age difference, are my role models.

Alex has been the one person who has endured through my long-term goal of putting these police stories to paper and print. I thank her for her unending encouragement, assistance and love. She is a true partner.

——— INTRODUCTION ———

"422 to 409."

"409, go ahead."

"If you want to stop by you can take some more photographs for us."

"No thanks, I've got other plans. Do you have enough help without me?"

"10-4."

———

I should have been thankful for the offer, instead it only reinforced my unwillingness to be a part of one more grisly scene of death. My shift was over. I had paid my dues. I just didn't have it in me to look at yet another dead teenager.

As I pulled into my driveway, only a mile from the fatal train-car wreck, I hadn't yet learned the identity of the deceased. Later, from the radio, I heard that the victim was the daughter of our school superintendent. But, even had I known the senior high school student, I might have still turned down the offer to help. My mind was elsewhere.

I was remembering a previous case where investigators continued to search a home for a suicide note. Their challenge was in determining if a fifteen-year-old boy, reportedly intoxicated, had died due to a self-inflicted .22 bullet to the head, and if so, attempt to determine if it was accidental or suicide. I knew from experience that despite a thorough investigation, we were sometimes never absolutely sure of the intentions of the deceased.

Meanwhile, declining the invitation to examine the wreckage at the railroad crossing did not free me entirely from the stress of police work. My memory bank began to automatically replay other cases I had helped investigate in my previous seven years working patrol.

On patrol ("the road") I was always tied to the police radio where at any moment one phone call from the public could disrupt ongoing work, a meal or a bathroom break. Dispatchers told us when and where to go. We were assigned to some emergency, nearby or distant, and we were off, red lights flashing, sirens wailing, in a hurry to get somewhere for somebody. Earlier in my career, I had been excited about the adventure of the unknown, but now this process no longer served my needs.

Patrol duties had begun to feel like an obligation, not a ball and chain scenario, but a short leash. Like every officer, I carried a handcuff key, but for me to be revitalized and remain in law enforcement, I needed to discover a key that could open up the best opportunity for my professional growth. It required a career plan adjustment that had not yet solidified in my mind.

I had started yearning for a scheduled shift that actually ended on schedule, where I would drive straight home, without an extra hour or two of duty because of late assignments and the predictable piles of paperwork. Our work would not wait and being tired was never an excuse, because each of us was a link in the chain of a professional organization. Serving the public was still vitally important to me. I just needed to be sure to serve myself and my family in the process. "Could I do all three?" was the ultimate question.

In the middle of all this uncertainty an unexpected door opened to a newly created position in our department. Because of my duty experience of giving programs in the schools, communicating with the teachers and connecting with the children, I was offered the position as our first school liaison officer. I was excited about the possibilities of my effect on children and I knew that the job would be good for me by putting some distance, some time, between deaths.

* * *

As our department's first School Resource Officer (SRO), I eagerly explored the unlimited possibilities. Youth development, decision-making and resistance skills quickly became areas of focus. Maybe, I reasoned, working with young people about problem-solving would help empower them to make better choices, so that law enforcement wouldn't have to problem-solve their deaths or crimes, be it at the scene of a motor vehicle accident, drug overdose, suicide or homicide.

Visiting the grade schools with the welcoming, curious children, who were sometimes shy but seemingly, rarely frightened, was a breath of fresh air. As much as I had enjoyed patrol, I felt like the new work gave me control and direction back in my life. Instead of rotating shifts, I had standard daytime hours. This regularity in scheduling school visits, the predictability of my day, along with the positive feedback of my contacts, made all the difference in my outlook. The change made me realize I had been under a lot of stress, if not close to burned out, working on the road. Even though I had never fought a war in a distant land, a professional opinion might have diagnosed that I had a case of post traumatic stress syndrome, not uncommon in police work.

My return to the helping field of teaching was ideal. I relished every educational encounter with the school children! Becoming an SRO allowed me to become who I already was, a mixture of law enforcement officer and educator. This opportunity to blend beliefs and experiences made me a stronger link in the Sheriff's Department as I again, passionately and proudly, served the public. Only this time I was focusing on its youth. It was an assignment that only got better.

1

QUESTIONS FROM KIDS

"IS YOUR GUN LOADED?"

"You have a gun in school! You're breaking the law!" I'm challenged by a grade school student—no doubt a future prosecuting attorney.

Sometimes adults, uncomfortable seeing me in my deputy sheriff's uniform, will hold up their hands and say, "I didn't do it!" But children in the comfort of their classroom will eagerly inquire about what it's like being a police officer, especially about my equipment. The most common question in grade school on my first visit: "Is your gun loaded?" It's a good question.

Categorically, questions about cops from kids tend to follow a developmental pattern based on their age or grade level. It would be fascinating for me to learn what motivates some of the inquiries. Does the nearly four-foot tall, five-year-old kindergarten student ask me, "Why do you have a gun?" because he or she is trying to sort out the concept of good and bad, right or wrong? If police officers are viewed as good and guns as bad then what value do I register in a young child's mind?

Is my gun the focus of attention due to a child's early exposure to gun safety from a memorable parental talk, or is it a result of the ever-present assault of violent images in the media? Is it due to the actual news on television or the more violent Saturday morning cartoons that have already planted this seed of fearful thought about violence? Has the child seen a real gun before or used a play one that morning to pretend to shoot someone? I, too, like a curious child, have so many questions I'd like to have answered.

I'm asked if I've ever been shot before or if I've shot anyone else. Clearly, wearing a gun to school is a big deal! I can see why kids that carry weapons get a lot of attention. I take the focus off my gun as soon as possible, but I use the generated interest as a way to make a point. My goal, always, is to get past the gun questions and answers so that once I've responded, I can give some safety advice. In the process, I try to convey that while I carry a gun I consider myself a *peace officer.*

Unlike a lot of conflicts created for action TV and suspenseful movies, most problems can be solved, and should be solved, without violence. We need to realize that solving conflicts is the process of finding a way to cope with dissatisfaction, unhappiness, and the stress of learning to live with anger, fear and disappointment. Ideally, a police officer, like anyone else, needs to be able to help people solve their problems without using a gun. It's a sad and scary day when anyone takes a gun out to try to hurt someone. But it's a fact of life and death.

Is my gun loaded? I often turn the question back to the children, "What do you think?" Half bet that there are bullets in the weapon. Others can't fathom that I, a police officer, would be breaking a school rule by bringing a gun inside their home away from home.

"Yes, it's loaded, because I'm on duty and if an emergency were to happen I'd want to be able to respond immediately. If someone were trying to seriously hurt or kill you or me I couldn't call time out. It's not a game. It's not make-believe. I'd do everything possible to talk the person into putting their weapon down and to not hurt themselves or others. But at some point, it's true, I might have to shoot, even kill them because of a dangerous choice they made. I hope I never have to. I became a police officer to help people. But if I ever take a life I want it to be because I saved my own life or the life of someone else in an attempt to make the world a better place."

Beginning in about fourth grade there's usually one needy student that will ask to see my gun. "Will you pass it around, please?" Then there is laughter with a nervous edge. They know I won't pass it around.

Instead, I ask them "What do you think would happen if I did? What would you do? How long do you think I'd have my job?'"

"You'd be fired today!"

"I'm here to talk about safety. Would it be a good idea to pass around a loaded gun?"

"No!" they shout in unison.

"Why not?" I continue.

"Someone might accidentally pull the trigger. We could get hurt."

"How do you think I would feel if during my talk on safety someone was hurt because I passed around my gun? How would your friends and family feel if you were injured or killed?"

In seconds I've turned the original question around for them to answer. Then I'll give them my own, standard, three-part answer.

"There are only three reasons I'd take my gun out of this safety holster.

"One. In an emergency where someone's life is at risk. When I say emergency, am I talking about people spilling their milk or running in the hallway? Do I mean that they called me a bad name or that they wouldn't show me their driver's license? I would only take out my gun if I were preparing to use it. Otherwise, everyone, including me, is safer with my gun in its holster.

"Two. To practice at the firearm's range, a place that is built to stop the bullets from accidentally hurting others. Would your backyard be a safe place? Where would it be safer? Why do I need to practice?" And I tell them that, like at school, we have training and tests, only our exams are to make sure we are good shots. If we don't pass the shooting qualification then we can't carry our gun. If we can't carry our gun we don't have our job. Do you want police officers that can make good decisions about when and when not to take their gun out and use it? Do you want officers that can shoot straight? What could happen if an officer wasn't a good shot?

"Three. To clean it, not play with it. I've never played with this gun, because it's not a toy. There are play guns and there are real guns. This is a real gun. If you have a toy gun then you should only be playing with it with your friends, not with strangers. Why should you never point even a toy pistol at someone you don't know, especially a police officer?"

Answers come quickly.

"They might not know it's a toy."

"They might think it's real!"

"We might get shot!"

"My gun is a tool I use in my job just as a carpenter uses a hammer or a saw," I continue.

"Even though I've never played with my real gun, I've enjoyed practicing with it. Like some of you today, I had toy guns when I was growing up."

I wonder if my playing with toy guns and pretending to be a marshal or deputy sheriff influenced me to eventually choose my job as a peace officer? As a child my television role models, the *Lone Ranger* being a favorite, were always defending the weak against some armed bandit or bully. It's a blessing that I found a career, which allows me to continue to work towards a goal of community justice. As an adult I still wear a tin badge, but now the badge is real, I have greater influence, and I get paid for my work! My weapon is no longer a toy six-shooter but a semi-automatic with sixteen rounds of ammunition. As an adult I know that the job is not glamorous like television shows, but it can be very stressful, occasionally dangerous, and usually rewarding.

Toys I played with in my childhood became the tools of my trade in my future. As proof, I still have a color photograph of myself when I was about six-years old, standing proudly with my toy pistols, cowboy hat, and, yes, a marshal's badge pinned on my cowboy vest! How did I know I'd be a deputy sheriff someday? I didn't, but at an early age the playing or pretending opened up the possibility in my head.

Sometimes I'll take a quick survey. "How many of you have a real gun in your home?" In our rural area schools I usually see at least half the students respond with raised hands. Then I ask them to explain what rules they are expected to follow when they're around guns. Whether parents realize it or not, the kids know where the guns in their homes are kept. Most of the homeowner weapons and ammunition are unsecured, protected only by the tenuous verbal warning from an adult to a child. And in urban communities, especially those in high crime areas, many kids, even those without a gun in the home, can get one cheaply and easily.

The belief which has been most detrimental to our young people is the concept that for their protection they are safer carrying a loaded gun than if they had no gun at all. This irrational thinking is easy to understand when you consider the millions of media messages they have received in their brief lifetime. One modern version of man's primitive fight or flight syndrome is to fight with the biggest gun or toughest gang and when fleeing is necessary, do it with the most expensive pair of tennis shoes, fastest car, or most powerful truck. And if you need to steal the truck, that's okay too. Just take it.

To the children I'll emphasize what every parent, especially those with weapons in the home, has already instructed; "Don't ever touch a gun without adult supervision." If I'm talking to a parent I'll inform them that guns kept in the home for personal safety are much more likely to harm a resident—themselves or children—than an intruder. I'll also preach the use of gun locks.

By the fifth grade I'll have students telling me about how they earned their hunter safety card and can now go hunting with adults, usually a parent. There's never enough classroom time, but occasionally I'll ask these hopeful hunters to share some gun safety tips with the class. Part of me is telling myself to avoid talking about guns. I don't want the kids to get too curious or the guns to be a status symbol. The other part of me is recognizing that a lot of the children are already past being curious and that I should use them as a resource to teach their peers respect for firearms and the importance of safety.

When I'm asked if I've ever been shot at, I usually reply, "Not that I know of!" Or if students want to know if I've have ever been shot, I tell them, "Yes." But I follow up, explaining that when I was growing up there was a boy in high school, three or four years older than me that purposely shot me a couple of times with a BB rifle. I guess he got bored killing the song birds sitting innocently enough on the telephone lines in our suburban neighborhood. Thinking back, I wonder if he ever progressed to a real gun with human victims, or was I just a bigger moving target one lazy summer day, when showing off to a friend and his brother became more important to him than common sense?

My childhood experience of being shot with a BB rifle is mild compared with many children today. In urban America, a discussion on guns can quickly lead to students showing their numerous wounds from gunfire and knife fights. The scars and actual accounts of friends and family members being shot and killed can make a police officer sit up and take notice. Imagine spending an entire childhood growing up in a war-torn neighborhood or country where guns and gunfire are part of the environment and atrocities are routinely committed on adults and children. For some, this describes a foreign country. For others it's called home.

2

MENTAL ILLNESS, POVERTY AND DOMESTIC VIOLENCE

"HAVE YOU EVER GOT IN A FIGHT ON DUTY?"

"If the only tool you have is a hammer, it is tempting to treat everything as if it were a nail." —Abraham Maslow[1]

"Dispatch to 431."

"431, go ahead."

"Maple Grove trailer court, lot 29, family disturbance. Calling party advises he is inside the trailer, his wife is outside in the vicinity. No weapons involved at this time."

"431, 10-4."

Another case that stands out from my early experiences on the road was a "family disturbance" call I was assigned to one afternoon. According to the woman I met as I pulled up to the address, she and her husband had been arguing and he had pulled her hair, pushed her against the wall and held her head against it with his forearm. To give him time to cool off, she and the two kids left for a walk. Upon her return she discovered her husband had locked them out of the trailer and he would not let her back inside. In control of the phone, he called us, the Sheriff's Department, before she did.

The woman told me that the children, two and five-years old, were presently at a neighbor's trailer being watched. She told me that she would not stay in the same trailer with her husband that night nor would she let the children remain with him. Her reasoning was that she didn't know if he would get angry and take it out on them. I immediately asked her if he had ever hurt the kids before and she responded that she "didn't know." Then she told me that she had been abused and pushed around by her husband off and on since the last family disturbance call about two months earlier, but that she "put up with it." I then asked her to wait at her neighbor's trailer with her kids while I spoke with her husband.

My shift sergeant arrived and we both talked with the husband in the trailer that he and his wife leased. He was nursing a cracked collarbone with one arm in a sling. The injury was from an earlier fight—only that encounter was with someone bigger and stronger than his wife. Our subject explained that he originally called us regarding a complaint against him by his landlord. He was being accused of speeding in the trailer court and he wanted us to know that he would "fire on the landlord if he starts in on me." Then the individual told us the real reason for the call. He explained to me how his truck had broken down and how his wife always blamed him for anything that went wrong. He also gave me a little background that both he and his wife were unemployed, on welfare and receiving food stamps. He blamed his wife for having him arrested in another state for assault and battery and that he had then been in jail for two weeks. He also willingly offered that he had been in the state mental hospital for over a decade. I didn't doubt it. Finally, in describing his version of the present accusation, he admitted to pushing his pregnant wife, "but didn't knock her down."

Back in these earlier days there were no laws, at least none normally enforced, that said an aggressor or batterer *must* be arrested and go to jail if the officer had reason to believe there had been violence in the home. If there was an angry verbal dispute, even physical fighting, then our main objective was to separate them and let them cool off. Sometimes we would leave them on their own, but preferably in the company of sympathetic family members or friends offering shelter and emotional support. There was no standard expectation that physical violence on either or both parties would—like today—automatically mean temporary confinement behind steel bars. The change in law is reflected in the very name of the calls. In the olden days it was a "family disturbance." Today it is "domestic violence."

In this case, the husband made it obvious to us that his wife could go where she wanted, but that the kids were going to stay with him. He was unwilling to let his wife and children remain at the trailer if it meant him leaving for the night. He made it perfectly clear to me that the kids were staying with him. I wondered though if this was due to his protective fatherly love, stubbornness, a mechanism of manipulation for controlling his wife by firmly grasping what was closest to her heart, or other socio-economic factors I hadn't yet considered?

In trying to come up with a temporary solution, my sergeant stayed with the husband outside their leased trailer while I returned to talk to his wife about his unwillingness to compromise. She wasn't surprised. She also firmly stated again that neither she nor the kids would spend the night with him. I then called a local spouse abuse representative who said they had money to put the mother and children up in a motel for the night. I told the advocate I'd call her back.

Being back in the days before cell phones, my sergeant left the scene for a nearby fire station in order to call the County Attorney for advice about the legal complications of both parents demanding their children remain with them. Before my supervisor could return, he was sent on another disturbance of higher priority, this one reportedly involved a gun. During his absence I attempted to set the scene for a reasonable resolution. I advised the husband of three choices he and his wife had: that his wife and kids could stay in town for the night without him, a juvenile officer could put the kids in a shelter home, or the kids and his wife could stay at her mother's until he and his wife could get along better. His response shocked me. He said that he would not let anyone take his kids and that "you better make your first bullet count." It seemed I still needed work on my negotiation skills. At this time he retrieved a homemade weapon, a nunchaku (two cut off pool stick handles attached together with a piece of rope) from his porch and passively held them in his available hand. On my walkie-talkie I radioed for Savior Sarge. When he asked me for an update I told him, "Things are quickly deteriorating."

The demanding dad told me that I had better call the reinforcements off! I declined. He said that he wanted to talk to his wife and I said okay, as soon as another officer arrived. He then approached me while holding, but not brandishing the nunchaku. The aggressor asked me if an officer had any business telling him how to run a marriage.

I replied confrontationally, "No, not unless one person is being abused and complains."

In our little give and take, he said, "Answer the question," and proceeded to walk towards me.

I wanted to avoid a physical fight with him, but my mouth got in the way. From the subject's first comment about firing on the landlord, I had been sizing up the situation. The winged warrior had a nonfunctional nunchaku. It looked like a heavy-duty jump rope for oversized Olympic wrestlers, but one end could have been swung at me with powerful and damaging force. On the other hand, I had a gun in my holster with six silver bullets. I didn't want a wrestling match, but if there was one, I was prepared to jump all over his injured collarbone. I wasn't too excited about any hand-to-hand combat, especially since I would need to protect my weapon during the scuffle, but under the circumstances I wasn't ready to shoot him, so I rejected the idea of taking my gun out. Choosing the most sensible, but certainly not a courageous choice, I simply moved to the other side of the patrol car putting it between him and me. He moved around the car one way and I kept an equal distance from him. Then we both just stopped. So, this was what the fleeing army called a tactical retreat. At an impasse, in the background I heard the welcome sirens of the mechanized cavalry coming, getting closer, reassuring me in spite of the unreasoning subject three yards away. To my opponent the sensory sirens simply offered another reason for yet another command: "Tell them to turn their sirens off!"

You can learn a lot about people by listening to their demands and observing their actions. His seemed irrational to me, but they could have very well been the survival skills he was forced to learn growing up in a dysfunctional family, as a victim of child abuse, yet another baby born into poverty, or simply symptoms of his mental illness. Or all of the above. I kept thinking from my limited point of view: "If I was in his shoes wouldn't I be more cooperative?" But my experiences and rules were different! I was thinking about my survival, considering what alternatives I had besides using deadly force. I wasn't comprehending the situation from his perspective. Here, I had a subject with a broken collarbone, one arm in a sling, and the other squeezing a jump rope, advancing on me, a uniformed, armed deputy. Did he want to get hurt or did he even care? This guy would go to a gunfight with a pocketknife! I had good reason to keep myself out of the rope's reach.

He had just created the justification for my
requested backup and now he was telling me
the sirens bothered him! I understood he was
likely thinking that his landlord would use the
emergency police presence as another reason to
send him packing, but I blamed him for creating
the dilemma, and I wasn't feeling charitable. As
the two patrol cars pulled up, seconds apart, I
was ready to cheer, but instead I kept my eyes
on the winged warrior and the neighbor's trailer
behind him. His wife had a front row seat. She
was watching the standoff.

As I glimpsed his wife looking out the
window, I wondered if the armed deputies she
requested were still the help she sought. She
wanted relief. Were we giving her grief? How
did she feel right now? Was she wondering if
we were going to arrest or hurt her husband,
and would this upset or please her? And,
while we prepared for offensive maneuvers,
were the changing circumstances cause for
her to attempt to rescue her husband from us?
Whichever side she took it was easy for me to
feel for this abused wife, since her demanding
husband was aggressive towards me, a sheriff's
deputy, what numbing or bruising encounters
had she endured for years? I thought I might
understand her reasoning for remaining in this
relationship. In the cycle of violence, after his
mean monster phase, he could no doubt be a
charmer and lover as though on a honeymoon.
He would make promises of peace as she dreamed
of cooperative change. But I couldn't grasp his
thinking. This man who had the shortest of
unstable fuses, who was potentially as deadly
as damaged dynamite, was literally waving red

flags in our faces. *"This,"* I thought, *"must be the face of mental illness."* Years later I included another explanation: his reasoning was part of the survival mode of generational poverty.

In seconds my Sarge took control of the situation. That day he was my hero. He checked with me on what had occurred in his absence. I told him I had not been threatened, but I had retreated for my strategic protection. Then, as three uniforms began to slowly circle this subject, Sarge quickly instructed the man to drop the nunchaku. The sergeant with stripes, unsnapped his holster, threatening to use his gun, but before I could learn if he meant it, we were told by our would-be-wrestler that he'd put down the nunchaku if we wouldn't surround him. Finally, he was making sense! It was our show of power, not words, that he understood.

The couple, man and wife, then talked together and agreed to work out their problem, with the woman agreeing to stay in the trailer with her husband and the children that evening. The belligerent bully had gotten his way, no doubt, again. We left, knowing that we'd be back another day. There were still so many unanswered questions. I wondered if down the road the husband would meet his maker at the hands of violence the same way he pushed people, including cops, to the brink, misjudging when to blink. And, what could I do to see that someday soon he would get therapy for what I perceived as his mental illness?

Today it's difficult to imagine the level of violence that may have occurred in the household while law enforcement was writing reports, not making arrests. Violence in the home clearly won over peace and justice that day. The standard belief at that time, at least in the world of law enforcement, was that married couples in their own residence had permission to engage in emotional and limited physical warfare. If there were no signs of injury to either party or if both persons were injured then, it was a toss up. That usually meant a written report with no one arrested and no charges filed.

That day, early in my career, when I didn't pull out my revolver (we weren't carrying pepper spray or Tasers yet), could have ended very differently had I been inclined to use lethal force. An investigation might have justified a shooting due to me being confronted by an aggressor threatening me with a weapon. But I would have forever known that my deadly reaction was premature, and partially due to my arrogant approach to people who thought and acted differently than me.

When I used my "parent voice," I was dictating to him what he *had* to do. I called them choices but I wasn't giving him any. I wasn't asking for his input to solve the problem because, I rationalized, I wasn't his counselor, I was a sheriff's deputy. I wasn't treating him as an equal or with respect because I was judging him by his behavior. I treated him as a powerless, helpless child and he responded accordingly.[2]

Had Dr. Ruby Payne, the leader in the field of understanding people in poverty, observed me using my "parent voice," telling the subject his three choices, she could have predicted my predicament![3] When had he ever, in his whole life, felt the power to make a real choice? Wasn't this just another fateful day where he felt he had no control over the outcome? While I was talking to him about his choices, I was able to picture the possible repercussions of each. I was accustomed to planning ahead. What was different in my life was that I found ways to be in control because of a strong framework of support including my ongoing educational success, financial and emotional well-being, and my positive relationships. He, on the other hand, with very few resources, didn't have a safety net. When I stumbled, I recovered. When he stumbled it was devastating. He felt forever trapped in a familiar corner or on the edge of a dangerous precipice where anger, denial and hopelessness were always just a thought away.

I had quickly recognized his unpredictability, but I had not understood that the only tool he had in his conflict resolution toolbox was a hammer. To him, I was a threat to his family and to his emotional balance. To him, in every passing minute I was looking more and more like a target. He held the hammer and I was the pesky nail that needed to be hit. My uniform and gun didn't matter one bit. When under stress he had run to his toolbox and found only a nunchaku. Ironically, once he was holding this symbolic hammer he might actually have been able to more easily predict the consequences of using it. Once he concretely held his nunchaku he may have understood that he finally had some real choices to make and that his next decision might land him in jail. He had to decide how far he was willing to go to maintain control over his most prized *possession*, his family. Could he fight himself out of yet another corner? It was dramatically clear to me that he felt cornered a lot.

The control he craved and created was derived from his physical confrontations. A broken collarbone was painful, but less painful than being told what to do by anyone, especially his wife or the police. In fact, in his neighborhood it was a sign of respect to survive jail. It gave one status. Those who ran from a fight risked losing social standing and were potential targets of disrespect.

Today I have a better understanding of his point of view. He was unemployed, living off food stamps. The trailer court manager was threatening to kick him and his family out of their home. His wife had recently got him locked up in jail. Now she was upset with him for being late when anyone could see it wasn't his fault the car broke down. This skinny cop had the nerve to butt into his personal business, to tell him how to treat his wife (his property) in the privacy of his own home and he hadn't even hit her! Now the cops were telling him he would have to give up his God-given right to be with his children when anyone could see that they were evidence, proof of his lover status. And besides, he had to hold onto his children, because they were the key to holding onto his wife.

When a man pushes around a woman, especially one that's pregnant, I take sides. I'm for the woman and unborn child. Sure, Mr. Nunchaku had plenty of problems. I had one too—him. I was judging him and he knew it. I didn't respect him. I wasn't willing to play what I saw as games, to be nice to perpetrators. I wasn't willing to be flexible. I wasn't neutral. The only empathy I was feeling was towards his wife and their baby-to-be. I wasn't willing to be one of the guys, implying that it was okay for him to push his wife around as though she were livestock. In no way was I willing to give him implicit permission to mistreat his wife, to take out his life of frustration on her.

Despite his actions, though, I never thought he was stupid. He was smart in getting what he wanted. To prove it, he survived that day without going to jail, to the hospital or the morgue. He had probably read me like a book from my first approach because he was always on hyper-alert, ready to fight for his survival. While I was judging him he may have already ascertained that I wasn't going to be a threat— until reinforcements arrived. Physical force was one thing he understood. It had been used on him or by him his entire life.

Ultimately, whatever approach I had taken that day, whether it was born out of arrogance or ignorance, might have had similar results. I was a police officer, an authoritarian figure from the middle class, and as a government representative I was enforcing the boundaries of what was deemed socially acceptable (middle class) behavior. He had other rules. We were two powerful forces and like two Siamese fighting fish, placed into a small bowl together, we were circling for the fight. Each of us was trained in force, looking for weaknesses in our opponent, recognizing the other as the enemy, but each lacking skills in understanding and negotiation.

That episode so many years ago concluded without violence, but no real problems were solved. Just a couple of weeks ago I saw the older Mr. Nunchaku in court. He was there in the audience watching his adult son get charged with battery. I wondered if that young man might have been the unborn baby I never met on the day I didn't have to shoot his father. It made me realize what a deep, complicated, ongoing problem I had been called to when I was a rookie officer.

3

COWARDICE OR COMMON SENSE

"HAVE YOU EVER BEEN PEPPER SPRAYED?"

"Do you carry pepper spray?"
"Did you ever pepper spray anyone?"
"Have you been pepper sprayed?"
"Is that pepper spray on your belt or is that your flashlight?"
"Will you show us your pepper spray?"
"What's in pepper spray?"
"Does it really burn your eyes?"
"Can a person see after they've been pepper sprayed?"

The questions that come quickly and confidently from the kids are probably the result of watching a lot of TV. I have very little firsthand information to share with them about struggling with violent offenders, but I can spice up my answers with accurate information from my training.

* * *

The officers on my shift were told that there would be training on "aerosol irritant projectors" and that after completing the half-day session we would be issued an aerosol can that held an organic agent derived from the cayenne pepper plant. This spray, classified as an inflammatory agent, would be yet another item to carry on our already bulging duty belt. The training would consist of a classroom portion and a hands-on-in-the-face finale in which we were asked to submit to being pepper sprayed.

I wasn't looking forward to the training, but I accepted it. The department was giving us an additional tool, a weapon that we would have at our disposal when we encountered violent behavior. Why wasn't I more appreciative? Under the right circumstances using pepper spray to control a violent subject could actually decrease the necessity of using lethal force. By pulling out our pepper spray instead of our gun the risk of great bodily harm to both the suspect and the officer decreases. When serious injury or death is preventable, that's clearly a win-win situation.

On the other hand, I wasn't looking forward to the temporary pain of being sprayed in my eyes, my most treasured gift. What if, despite all the assurances that the irritant would wear off within an hour somehow, on me, it didn't? What if the capsicum in my can had an unsafe level of ingredients and I had *willingly* invited damage to my nerve fibers or corneas? Some officers would prefer to be engaged in a gunfight than to be assigned to a public speaking engagement. I was thinking that performing in front of an audience was a breeze compared to the risk and prospective pain of being pepper sprayed.

Call it fear or call it common sense, I just didn't see the necessity of submitting to this agonizing encounter when I wasn't the criminal. We carried a gun and we weren't asked to be shot to see what it felt like, I reasoned. Instead we received firearms training and were required to qualify four times a year at the shooting range, firing at inanimate objects that didn't return fire using live rounds.

Apparently, the reason for being sprayed was that once we experienced the burning sensation we would then be less likely to misuse the weapon. Also, if we sprayed someone in the eyes we would understand the importance of getting the suspect to a source of water. That way they could flush their eyes out with large amounts of the clear, cool liquid. Okay, I promised myself, I'd take seriously the use of this new tool on my belt. I wouldn't spray anyone without due cause and I would never use it "in a punitive, retaliatory, vengeful, or indiscriminate manner."[4]

As I prepared myself psychologically for this uncomfortable training I overheard some officers who had already taken the schooling. They remarked that it was optional to be sprayed. Optional? What were they talking about? It immediately got me to thinking about a different possibility. I quickly learned that although it was a choice, all the officers in the first training group had voluntarily suffered through the incapacitating ordeal.

In life, including your job, you always have choices. It sounded like I could participate in the training but decline being pepper sprayed without it resulting in my reassignment, loss of pay or being fired. But I wanted to find out more about the consequences of not going along with the crowd in blue. I checked with my direct supervisor and learned that being sprayed was, in fact, optional. Then I started considering the potential fallout from standing out in a crowd of my peers. How would my choice affect me in my group of deputies? How would they treat me differently? Would I lose their confidence or respect? Would my action be seen as cowardice and result in officers questioning my level of competence and commitment if they needed backup? And finally, how important to me was their opinion?

I chose to listen to my instinct and to not worry about what someone else might think of me. I chose to *not* be pepper sprayed. My ego was up to it. I was comfortable in my decision and no one said anything to me about it. Ultimately, it wasn't a big deal.

At the hands-on training in the gymnasium, filled with fellow officers, I had the opportunity to test my aim and the propellant's power as a classmate advanced toward me acting aggressive. With pinpoint accuracy I watched the stream of foam approach and hit my partner's eyes, then observed him change from an aggressive assailant to a confused, submissive victim, all within one to two seconds. He was no longer a threat. The stuff really worked!

In the process of officers spraying one another and being helped to the bathroom sinks for copious amounts of cool water to be flushed into their eyes, I learned another reason to suffer the consequences of the realistic training. Each of the officers who participated through the panic of burning eyes and temporary blindness learned firsthand that they could survive the ordeal. This would be crucial information if down the road they were the target—purposely or accidentally—of their own hot pepper propellant. It could save a life.

I learned another lesson during the training. We all participate to different degrees. While in the bathroom watching half the officers urgently trying to restore their vision, I observed one combatant who was only *pretending* to be in pain. He had chosen to be deceptive, to act as if the foam had reached his face when in reality it had missed its mark. He had not received a discharge of the aerosol, but as an accomplished actor, had grabbed his eyes in reaction to the burst. This performer avoided the burning sensation, the temporary visual impairment, and any potential negative peer pressure that he might have incurred, had the group realized his degree of non-participant status.

He, like me, had made a choice to opt out only he did it with less risk of being judged by his peers. It was a reminder. We each do what we need to do and we do it in our own way.

* * *

Back in the classroom, my memories in tact, I begin to answer the flood of questions from the fourth grade students.

"Yes, I carry pepper spray.

"Yes, I've pepper sprayed an officer during our training, but I have not, so far, sprayed anyone violently breaking the law.

"No, I haven't been pepper sprayed. I had the opportunity, but I declined after considering the consequences of what others might think of me.

"No, I won't take the pepper spray out, because I'm not planning on using it. It's safer for everyone if I keep it on my belt. The can looks like any other regular aerosol can only it has a flip top cover guarding the button that you press down.

"The ingredient in pepper spray that makes most people's eyes seem to burn is actually from the cayenne pepper plant. A really, really small amount of this pepper is mixed with a lot of water, alcohol, and a bonding agent to allow the ingredients to mix. This liquid is propelled out of the aerosol can by using nitrogen.[5]

"The pepper spray causes a sensation of burning to the exposed area of skin and will usually cause inflammation of the eyes, but it does not actually burn them.[6]

"Nearly everyone who is exposed to the pepper spray feels this burning sensation and inflammation which results in involuntary closure of the eyes. When people have their eyes either shut or heavily irritated then they aren't going to have the capacity to be very alert to their surroundings, at least temporarily. We've been told that the affected time is a half hour to forty-five minutes. From what I've seen, that's accurate.

"I've used cayenne pepper before on my food, but I assumed that pepper spray was a relatively new tactical weapon in fighting. Actually, red peppers were used 4,000 years ago when China and India were at war with one another. Soldiers ground up the peppers and wrapped the fine powder in rice paper. Then, at the right moment they'd set the paper on fire and launch it at the enemy troops. This created panic and difficulty seeing, which resulted in an unfocused fighting force.[7] Today, officers still must consider the weather conditions before deciding to use the inflammatory agent. Spraying an aerosol irritant projector into the wind can make an attempted arrest a whole lot more complicated and dangerous than it needs to be!"

4

BEING APPRECIATED OR NOT

"HAVE YOU EVER SAVED SOMEONE'S LIFE?"

"422, Dispatch."
"422."
"10-6 with PD at the attempted suicide."
"10-4, 422."

Occasionally, a young student will ask me if I've ever saved someone's life. I know that they're thinking about a specific life and death moment where my intervention shifted the circumstances in such a way that death was delayed to wait another day. Despite my perceived understanding of the question, sometimes I'll tell the questioner that every time I arrest a drunk driver my action may save at least one life or prevent a serious injury. Who's to say whether the driver I've stopped would have driven home safely had I not intervened? And maybe an arrest will be a driver's wake up call to make safer, saner choices in the future.

I could tell the students that over the years I've encouraged youth to remain drug-free, taught resistance skills and provided a mental model of non-violence problem solving. Yes, I could tell them about my efforts, but that's not what they want to hear. Day-to-day information about prevention and youth development work doesn't compare with action-packed police movies. Luckily, I have at least one story to share with them about intervening when a despondent man wielded a butcher knife in his home.

* * *

One night on third shift, while on patrol, I overheard Dispatch assigning city police officers to an attempted suicide in progress. Even though I was a sheriff's officer I realized I was reasonably close to the location, so I advised them I'd also be responding in case they needed assistance.

Upon my arrival there were already three officers present in the basement of the townhouse. In between the dead silence and eerie moans I soon learned that a man was periodically stabbing himself in the chest with a butcher knife. I could see the subject on the dirt floor of the crawl space lying on his side. The officer closest to the suicidal subject was talking to him, telling him he was there to help. The other officers were waiting for any change in the status quo.

When I asked the police department's sergeant about their plan I was told that his commanding officer, back at the station, had given them a direct order to not enter the crawl space as long as the individual was armed or a threat to others. This made procedural sense in regard to officer safety, but at the same time it seemed too restraining. I felt that while the lead officer was occupying the subject's attention there was a very good opportunity for someone else, with little risk, to approach the prone figure from his blind side and to disarm him. This plan seemed reasonable because every few seconds, after the man stabbed himself, he would thrust the knife into the ground before momentarily releasing it.

I quickly realized that as a sergeant, the ranking officer on duty for the Sheriff's Department, I had the authority to make my own command decision. The Police Department's policy didn't affect me and its ranking officers saw no reason to keep me from participating. Also, it was a quiet night in the county and I figured this wouldn't take very long. It didn't.

In getting prepared to enter the cramped quarters I decided that my helmet, while helpful at a riot, presented a problem of clearance with the low-lying ceiling of floor joists. I took it off. While today most officers would put on protective gloves at the first drop of blood, back then we weren't aware of the risks of blood-borne pathogens. I had no gloves to put on.

Unlike some previous crises scenes, time did not appear to be passing in slow motion for me. I was aware of having laser sharp focus. My visual perception appeared to be functioning flawlessly. Just minutes on site, I was already creeping towards the moaning man, my attention sharply focused on the arc and timing of the moving knife. Color coded, my partner in brown and I in blue understood each other through our body language. It was a simple plan. Silently, consciously breathing, I approached the focal point while my collaborator increased the volume of his chatter to the suicidal citizen.

When I was close enough and the subject had again forcefully stabbed the carving knife into the dirt, I reached for it, pulled it out, and in a fluid motion flung it to the other side of the crawl space, a good twenty feet from us. Then, as the subject frantically searched with his right hand for his slicing instrument, my partner and I grabbed his legs and pulled him out of his cramped quarters, making sure that no other weapons materialized to interrupt the momentum of our mission. Other officers soon joined in, assisting in controlling the bleeding body for the responding EMS crew who were just seconds away. Outside, beside their ambulance in the driveway, they'd been waiting for the all clear signal in order to enter the premises.

I returned to my supervisory responsibilities as the emergency medical technicians were examining the desperate subject before they transported him to the emergency room. The whole event seemed to be over before it started. My total time out of the car wasn't any longer than a short coffee break.

Back in my patrol car, alone again, I had a moment of euphoria, a rush, and I liked it! The rest of the shift I reflected on how easily and quickly the case had progressed. I was also left wondering what circumstances had caused this disturbed individual to go into such a personal crisis. At the scene all I'd been told was that he had had a fight with his mother.

* * *

Two days after my assist I received a call from a nurse at the hospital. She told me that the hospitalized man was doing well and would recover. Then she asked me if I had gotten any blood on my hands, and if so, did I have any open cuts, had I touched my eyes, ears or nose with any of the victim's blood. It was then I was informed that the hospital had discovered that their patient had a contagious blood-borne disease. "No, I don't think so," was my answer. But as a precaution I was encouraged to begin receiving a series of shots.

Despite the serious news I was able to find humor in it. Up to the time of her call no one had made a big deal about my help at the emergency. Weakly, I admitted to myself that I would have welcomed some recognition for the good work. But there's a saying to be careful what you wish for. With the nurse's call I got attention all right. It led me to the doctor's office on three occasions where I would drop my drawers in order to get a shot in my buttock. Instead of a *medal* pinned on my chest the only *metal* I received was in my behind.

But the greatest reward was my self-satisfaction in knowing that I responded appropriately in a life and death circumstance. I had helped save a life.

5

Be Careful What You Wish For

"HAVE YOU EVER ARRESTED A DRUNK DRIVER?"

"431, Dispatch."
"431, Go ahead."
"431, Dispatch, I'm following a possible 10-46 at K-96 and Blanchard in South Hutchinson. Stand by for tag number and direction of travel."
"10-4, 431."

———

Does every patrol officer remember his or her first arrest of a drunk driver? I remember mine. It was in the days before any preliminary breath test or intoxilyzer machine was used to determine a driver's blood alcohol level.

* * *

After two weeks on midnights, finally by myself, I had already assisted a couple of officers on DUI arrests, but I was anxious to initiate the process on my own. Now I was wishing for one. I'd been searching the darkness between my building checks in the outlying towns. I kept thinking, *"Where are they? Why can't I find a drunk driver?"*

In fishing you get nibbles. On patrol you get clues. For me, every moving vehicle held a potential intoxicated driver to catch and arrest. I'd been watching for the signs of a drunk or drugged driver: driving left of center or straddling lanes, weaving, driving extremely slowly or too fast, varying speed, disobeying stop signs and traffic lights or misjudging where to stop, poor turning, driving with no lights or failing to dim lights, and the most obvious—driving the wrong way on a divided highway.

I first observed my suspicious vehicle at 4:45 a.m. It was about four feet left of center, *approaching* my marked unit! I still hadn't learned to be careful what I wished for. As it passed by I turned around and followed the taillights. The car was weaving and going across the center line again. I was eager to pounce, but I wanted my body to catch up with my racing mind. Also, with no other traffic in the area, I felt it was safe enough to give the possible DUI a little fishing line. I wanted to make sure the driver was well hooked with solid evidence so that later he wouldn't get away in court.

I caught up to the suspect vehicle after it had stopped and waited at a stop sign for about thirty seconds. With no other traffic present I wondered about the reason for the delay. It seemed like forever before it started moving. Then, after it drove two blocks it stopped again, about five feet past a second stop sign. It remained there a prolonged minute before I'd seen enough. That's when, red lights flashing, I drove up behind the vehicle and officially made the traffic stop, calling in to dispatch our final location and complete tag number.

Excited, I approached the car and observed a man in the driver's seat with his head leaning forward—almost to the steering wheel. He appeared to be unaware of my presence outside his window. Sitting next to him on the passenger side was a woman who identified herself as his wife. The driver looked up at me with bloodshot eyes. I detected the familiar odor of an alcoholic beverage emanating from inside his vehicle. After I requested to see his driver's license the driver felt his pockets, apparently looking for his license and then stated that it was in the trunk. With the car's engine turned off, I invited him to get out and show it to me, figuring this would be a great sobriety test for balance. He exited the vehicle slowly and swayed to the rear of the automobile.

Despite the headlights of my patrol unit and the flashlight of a recently arrived back up officer, my suspected drunk driver had difficulty finding the correct key and in locating the trunk's keyhole. But, after numerous attempts, his body wobbling back and forth, he finally got the trunk to open. At that point the assisting officer recovered the wallet for him since we didn't want our suspect to be grabbing a stashed weapon to use on us or on himself.

I gave the subject some field tests including an alphabet test, coin test, and heel-to-toe test. He said the alphabet from "a" to "j" with some hesitation and obvious slurring. After the letter "j" he stopped and would not continue.

Next, I took a quarter, nickel, and dime from my pocket, and placed the group on the ground.

I asked him to pick the coins up, tell me how much money there was, and hand them back to me. He picked up the change as he swayed some, said there was "about forty-five cents," and dropped the dime before handing me the rest.

In response to my question about whether he had been drinking, he replied, "a few beers." After that I asked him if he knew about what time it was and he said "one o'clock" (when it was nearly 5 a.m.). When I inquired if he knew where he was he said, "Here. I'm right here." Then, after asking him if he knew what town he was in he hesitated, unsure, even though he lived only blocks away.

On the heel-to-toe test I explained and demonstrated it. He was talkative during this part of the exam and on two occasions threw his arms up in the air. I had instructed him to take seven steps forward and six back, but he was only able to take four steps forward, none heel-to-toe, before quitting and remarking: "I don't think anyone can do this test!"

I told the suspect that he was under arrest and asked him to take a blood alcohol test (BAT). He said, sure, he'd take the test because he wasn't drunk. I then field searched him, patting him down for weapons, explaining that in order to go to the hospital by patrol car I would need to handcuff him. He replied uncooperatively: "No one is going to handcuff me!" That's when my assisting officer and I looked at each other, rolled our eyes and took a deep breath. Ready for a struggle, we were surprised how little force was necessary to handcuff him. He was all talk.

We then placed him in my patrol car (in those days in the front passenger seat) and I drove him to the hospital for the BAT, while my back-up officer gave the arrestee's wife a ride home. Upon arrival at the emergency room I read the suspect his Miranda Rights. He said he'd heard them before and understood them. After he signed a consent form and the medical technician had drawn blood, my handcuffed prisoner and I headed to jail.

At the detention center the jailer processed the suspect and I asked him more questions. He said that he had been "drinking a six-pack or two," had started drinking after work at about 5 p.m. and had stopped about an hour before his arrest. He also informed us that he was under a doctor's care and that he was on medication— dilantum—as he was epileptic!

As I reviewed the traffic stop, BAT, and processing for my report I marveled at the range in emotions in this individual during the last hour. He had been talkative, combative, stupefied, insulting, and polite. He swayed and staggered while standing and walking. His speech was fair at times and slurred at other times. The effect of alcohol appeared extreme and his ability to drive was definitely impaired.

Days after the arrest the hospital informed our agency that the suspect's BAT had revealed a blood alcohol level of .32%, over three times the legal .10% level (four times today's .08% level).

* * *

I had my share of drunk driver arrests over the following six years, with the 11 p.m. to 7 a.m. shift yielding the greatest number, although intoxicated drivers are on the road at any hour. We even had one person, arrested in the middle of the day, who thought he'd avoid another DUI arrest by drinking a large quantity of really awful tasting mouthwash. A search of his stopped vehicle revealed a large, empty bottle of the popular germ-killing rinse. We confiscated it as evidence.

The arrestee never did admit to drinking anything but his mouthwash. If that was really true, with the small amount of alcohol content in the commercial product, we wondered how much he had to consume to be legally drunk. We never did the math and we never quite believed him.

* * *

There was the driver I stopped and after requesting to see his driver's license he said, "I don't have one. I'm from California."

* * *

The lady who was obviously drunk who, after failing the sobriety tests said out of nowhere, "I'm not crazy." Later she revealed, "I know the Sheriff's been following me for the last two months." In addition, her changing moods— from crying to screaming—could have been the result of the alcohol, mental illness or the sobering fact that this was her third DUI arrest. She tested .299%, three times the then current benchmark .10% blood alcohol level.

* * *

The driver who pulled his car over after seeing my patrol unit's emergency lights. As he exited his car I saw that his hands were empty, but his pockets were not. One had a brown paper sack that held an open pint bottle of 97 proof whiskey. This forty-one-year-old driver was the one who, at the jail during my further questioning, was asked when he had started drinking. While I had meant what time of the day, he replied, "I've drunk all my life."

* * *

The sixteen-year old who was stopped at 3:30 in the morning for erratic driving. When he got out of the vehicle he grabbed a small plastic bag out of his pocket, threw it in the air, and because of its light weight and the wind direction, it sailed upwards, then landed about five feet from where we were standing. Unprompted by me, he immediately said, "It's not my marijuana."

* * *

The fellow who thought he'd escape an arrest by not stopping for me until he had made it home, into his private driveway. Upon finally making contact with him he told me that he was on his own property and I couldn't do anything. He told me he was going inside. But instead, he submitted to some sobriety tests with his cowboy boots on the wrong feet, all the while denying any irregularity under foot! It was humorous, yet again, sobering. I placed him under arrest. He wasn't laughing when he responded: "You just made a mistake that's going to cost you."

He told his wife, who was on the front porch, awakened by my late-night, early-morning screaming siren, to call his good friend the Sheriff. She replied "that wouldn't be right."

Before leaving the scene I rechecked the truck's front seat area to see if there were any open containers of alcohol. I didn't find any beer cans, but under a bag of potato chips I recovered a loaded .22 handgun. Suddenly, I felt a chill in the warm summer air. I was relieved that the driver hadn't chosen to use his weapon, just an arm's reach away, on me. I emptied and confiscated the twenty-two, unclear at the time if the law permitted me to charge him with carrying a concealed weapon.

On the way to jail the arrestee told me that I could still let him go, that it would be worth it to me. He further informed me that I had made the biggest mistake of my career, because he and the Sheriff were good friends. My response was that he was welcome to call my boss after being booked into jail on his DUI charge.

During the paperwork process the drunken cowboy eagerly showed me his Fraternal Order of the Police membership card and named his circle of police friends. I wasn't impressed. When the last form was completed at 2 a.m. he was offered his phone call. He declined to contact anyone, not even the Sheriff, but he did have some parting words for me.

My prisoner offered me his hand to shake. I hesitated, but I knew I had to take this minor risk. Here was a human gesture I couldn't refuse. Maybe my professionalism (treating him respectfully and not taking things personally) had paid off. He was more than a DUI catch. He was a person who had possibly recognized that making threatening comments was unproductive. Maybe he was ready to accept responsibility for his temporary incarceration with no hard feelings towards me. I couldn't let the opportunity pass. Our eyes met. I held out my hand. Then, just as our palms touched, he leaned over to me and whispered "I'm after your ass now!"

One of the jailer's got up to take my prisoner to a cell. We were done. From the book-in counter I picked up my metal traffic book holder and glanced at my comforting quotation taped on its top, and calmly walked away. It was with me on every traffic stop and arrest. Before I approached every driver I was reminded: "Each of you must be quick to listen, slow to speak, and slow to be angry. For a man's anger cannot promote the justice of God."[8]

LIVING DEATH

"DID YOU HAVE TO SEE ANYBODY DIE BEFORE?"

Rrriinngggg!
"Patrol, Potter."
"We have a two vehicle, 10-40, on US 50, near Sylvia. Other units responding."
"OK. We'll go 10-8."

———————

My patrol sergeant and I were together at the station one misty morning when a report of a "10-40," fatality accident, was broadcast, sending us to the western portion of our county over twenty miles away. It was one of my first hot runs and I carefully but quickly pushed our emergency vehicle through the thick fog while my supervisor cranked up the radio, leaned back, and deeply inhaled his cigarette. Part of me wondered what the hurry was since we had officers closer to the scene, and the person was already dead. But I kept quiet. Upon arrival it was clear that there were a lot of responsibilities for us at the site, including preventing more accidents, especially from the drivers with their heads turned our way, unfocused from their own driving, examining the remains of the explosive two-vehicle wreck.

After assisting with measurements I was delegated to be the officer, with coaching, to do the interview of the pickup driver who had apparently driven left of center, colliding head on with the eastbound car. Since there were five people injured with cuts and bruises, our interviews took place at the closest hospital, which was outside of our county.

Standing out in my memory of the accident scene was the unusual way my sergeant stared at the deceased. He said: "Get over here and look at her." He told me afterwards, "It was good to get the first one out of your system because you never know how someone is going to react." Did he mean *out* of my system or *into* my system?

When I walked over to the body she didn't look severely injured considering the car's massive damage. It looked to me like it had been hit by a train! The extensive field of scattered debris reminded me of pictures of plane crash sites. As I stared at the corpse, still a person to me, all I could think of doing was to say a prayer for her. But I made sure not to close my eyes or bow my head. I wasn't being evaluated for my spiritual side. The department had a roster of volunteer chaplains available upon request and I wasn't looking to fill their shoes. I wanted to learn the ropes of a patrol officer which meant complying with the sergeant's order.

While working the fatality accident I was told that not only did we need to have a blood sample taken from the surviving driver but also of the deceased driver. I recall the emotional shock and sadness of the death to those involved. Interviewing witnesses meant I also talked with the young son of the injured driver about his observations. I couldn't tell what he was thinking. I wondered, *"Did he feel in some way responsible? Did he think his father was going to jail?"* He was silent, surely traumatized. What do you say to your father after experiencing a death ride with him? I also interviewed the survivors from the other vehicle, family members of the deceased. They had planned a vacation—not a tragedy, not a nightmare.

Afterwards, I wondered if I had been intrusive with the physically and emotionally injured. I'd done my job, but the death hadn't bothered me as much as I had expected. Since our county had been having a rash of fatalities, other officers told me that the worse ones were those with small children and people you knew. Maybe that explained why this death wasn't affecting me much. Or maybe I'd have a delayed reaction? I'd always thought of myself as a sensitive person. Now I was wondering if this was callousness or some natural, protective shield to personally and professionally guard me from the stressors of anxious encounters. The answer was a year in the future. I hadn't seen someone die, yet.

* * *

A year out of the academy, I was feeling confident. In spite of all the fatality wrecks, unattended deaths, and suicides our department was working, I hadn't had an inordinate amount on my shift or occurring on my beat. Few were "mine," in the sense that I was the assigned officer, from first showing up to working my way through the entire investigation. Homicides were quite different. They occurred rarely and they required a team effort due to the processing of the crime scene, necessity of extensive interviews and multiple leads to follow up quickly. However, my feeling of psychological well-being was short lived. My naivety was forever altered one night on third shift.

No fatality accident or wreck affected me as emotionally as the one I worked just a year out of the academy. The difference between viewing a corpse and watching someone die was indescribable. The feeling of helplessness and hopelessness was all consuming.

I can still clearly recall the event today. It was 1:09 a.m. on a holiday weekend. I was in my patrol car, checking the Brown Wheel tavern's parking lot when dispatch assigned me to a 10-48, injury accident, south of US 50 on Yoder Road. I was advised that the jaws of life, the fire department's hydraulic rescue equipment for extrication, had been requested. I knew I was the closest officer and wondered what I could do with anyone severely trapped in a vehicle. The best I could muster was a crow bar in the trunk. Useless. Four minutes later, at 1:13 a.m., I arrived.

It was pitch black. There were passersby already stopped, Good Samaritans. Partially on the roadway was a blue BMW sports car severely damaged on the front driver's side. *"How bad are the people hurt and what did this car hit?"* I thought. Before locating the second vehicle, I observed that the driver of the BMW was still behind the wheel. A Good Samaritan explained that the operator's legs were pinned in the vehicle. Sure enough, my flashlight confirmed.

I wasn't a doctor but it was obvious that the trapped driver was in critical condition, bleeding from the nose, mouth, and eyes, with labored breathing. I'd *never* seen anyone bleeding from their *eyes*! The driver's wife was lying on the ground beside the car with a blanket around her. She was conscious, some bleeding to her face, with another citizen volunteer beside her. The injured wife wanted to know if her husband was going to be alright. I tried not to show my fear as I told her, "We're helping him now."

My perception of time had slowed way down, but a couple of minutes later—it seemed like forever—I realized the other vehicle, a red pickup, was upright and well off the road some hundred feet away. It also had extensive damage to the front driver's side but not as extreme as the sports car. The windshield was damaged and partially pushed out. Behind the wheel was a young man. He was conscious, with blood on his face. The impact had trapped his leg in his vehicle as well. I asked him how he was doing and he acknowledged me.

I returned to the BMW where I checked on the driver, hoping we could get him out, but his feet were so confined in the metal cage of wreckage that movement of his head and shoulders was the extent of his freedom. He swayed rhythmically back and forth, slowly, as though instinctively he knew he was caught in a trap and needed to escape for his survival. Even though his body was moving he was never conscious. He didn't talk but gurgled. I said a few words to the severely injured man, quietly telling him that we were there to help and to hang on. As I looked for a way to assist, checking the extent of his bleeding, my prayers were not answered. Examining his head with the beam of my flashlight, I saw his right ear framed in its bright rays just before blood began flowing from inside, swirling, filling its cavity. Before my eyes he was dying from internal bleeding. *"How could he be saved?"* I wondered.

The first ambulance arrived four minutes after me, at 1:17 a.m., and began helping the injured. The most critical, the BMW driver was administered oxygen, an IV, attachments for monitoring vitals, and eventually electric shock to attempt to restore life. Attempts by emergency personnel operating the jaws of life, to extricate the driver from the vehicle were unsuccessful prior to his death. Due to the critical condition of the driver and the degree to which he was pinned in his vehicle, despite the team effort, he soon died. I remember that the EMT announced on the radio to Dispatch that one person had "expired." Our department used another term. In ten code the "10-48" injury accident had become a "10-40." Less than an hour later, at 2:27 a.m., the coroner arrived at the scene and examined the body of the deceased.

I had learned from one citizen who helped at the scene that she had opened the BMW's passenger door and the female inside had "collapsed out of the door." The Good Samaritan advised me she had discovered that the injured passenger and driver had been married earlier in the evening in Hutchinson and were on their way to Wichita. Later I learned that Wichita was to be the first leg of their honeymoon trip to Hawaii. But at the crash site, after hearing they had just left the wedding reception, I tried to make sense of it all. I figured that there was a good chance they had been drinking alcohol at the party.

Whether the groom was legally intoxicated or not, did not alter the facts at the scene. The road clearly showed that the northbound Ford pickup and the BMW had left a distinct gouge in the pavement more than four feet left of center into the BMW's southbound lane. This point of impact (POI) was as crucial to a motor vehicle accident investigation as the discovery of the location of the point of origin in a fire investigation. It explained the deep, head-on impact to both vehicles. But, while there were tire marks, I was surprised about the lack of brake marks.

After the injured were transported separately to the hospital and the deceased driver extricated from his car, our investigation of the traffic scene, using flashlights and headlights, continued. My sergeant helped reconstruct what had happened with the two vehicles from the moment of their deadly impact. We knew that two powerful colliding forces always tell a story. Between the damage to the vehicles, lack of brake marks, tire and skid marks, the POI, and debris, the story unfolded.

To confirm what the vehicles and roadway told us, we desperately wanted to interview the surviving driver, passenger, and any witnesses. At 3:10 a.m. I arrived at the hospital and received permission to speak with the injured driver of the pickup. He was lying on the examination table with dried blood on his face, stitches to his chin and a splint on his leg. His eyes appeared bloodshot. He agreed to let the hospital take a blood alcohol test.

At sunrise my sergeant and I were back at the scene of the wreck. We needed to examine the collision site in daylight to review measurements and take additional photographs. As the sun's illumination announced the new day, I could still sense the shapes and sounds from the darkness even though the broken vehicles and broken people were gone. What remained were scattered bullets of windshield glass and pieces of chrome. The pavement survived the deadly night's ordeal with only a grazing surface wound while the travelers in their modern metal machines, each with hundreds of horsepower, were not as fortunate. As two men in blue walked the tall weeds, looking for additional clues, we were surprised to find the hood of the truck some one hundred feet north of the crash site! In all the commotion and darkness neither of us had noticed the gigantic gap on the hoodless heap. I wondered, *"What else had we missed?"*

Later in the day, at 12:30 p.m. I continued our investigation back at the hospital. With the approval of the RN, I was able to meet the injured female, not only a passenger on a fatal ride but a victim; no longer the recent bride but a recent widow. In fair condition, with purple colored bruises surrounding both eyes and an injured left leg that wouldn't require surgery, she met with me for a second time. Her parents were present. I paid my regrets to all. *"How could this have happened?"* was the unspoken question we all asked.

After my condolences I proceeded delicately with the standard investigative questions. She remembered her husband having only one drink at their reception and that was a glass of champagne from a wedding toast. Also, she recalled that her husband had tea to drink with the meal and that he had advised her earlier that they should avoid alcohol.

The young widow, twenty-six, vaguely remembered turning onto Yoder Road, but said that she was either nearly asleep or knocked unconscious at the time of the accident. She said the first thing she recalled after the wreck was lying on the ground with a lady talking to her to keep her calm. She didn't know the speed of their car at the time of the wreck, but advised that her husband usually set his cruise control at 55-60 miles per hour. The BMW was hers and just a month old.

After fifteen minutes I left and walked down two floors where I again met the driver of the pickup, also in fair condition. With the permission of the nurse I explained to the nineteen-year old that I was required to complete the traffic accident form for the state. He said he was willing to talk to me, but that he couldn't tell me what happened because he couldn't remember. He recalled memory bits: being with some friends and leaving from there, and that he "came to" at the scene of the wreck.

At this point I explained to the young man that I was going to ask him some questions about alcohol and that I was going to read him his Miranda Rights again. When I finished he said he understood them. He admitted to drinking before the accident but "not much." He said he had four or five 3.2 (percent of weight by alcohol) beers while at the party.

Later, I learned that his BAC, the percentage weight of alcohol in the bloodstream, taken about two hours after the wreck had occurred, was determined to be .113%. This was at a time when the legal limit for those eighteen and over was .10%.

To my surprise, the BAC of the deceased was .000%. But it made sense. He had reportedly had a glass of champagne about 9 p.m. that within an hour and a half would have showed no discernible sign of alcohol registered in his blood. His body could have been free of alcohol for over four hours prior to the fatal wreck.

A week after my accident report was completed and turned over to the County Attorney's Office, a felony complaint of involuntary manslaughter was filed against the driver of the truck, contending that he was driving while intoxicated. At the time of this case the charge was a Class E felony, the least severe felony class of crimes. The maximum penalty upon conviction was five years in prison and a $5,000 fine.

That motor vehicle accident case was a great emotional and psychological burden for me. At the deadly scene I gave more time to the victims than I did the suspect. I got caught up in trying to save a life and ignored my responsibility to investigate the scene once enough emergency personnel were present. I was no EMT, but I had wanted more than anything to help this man live, even if my contribution was only holding a spotlight for the ambulance and fire department teams. When he died part of me died. Thankfully, I didn't attend the autopsy.

There was no preparation in my law enforcement training for watching someone "expire," but in looking back, there was an early clue. It was when my cigarette smoking sergeant on our fatality wreck run had recognized the enormity of an officer's first official encounter with death. At the scene he had ordered me to go over there and look at the body. He had been preparing me for what would be worse, still yet to come. Like a mother fox with her young he was conditioning me to a harsh environment and allowing me to practice my survival skills while he was nearby looking over my shoulder, ready to push me forward and encourage me if I hesitated.

My experiences with death were just part of the job, but boy, they've sure stayed with me a long time! My memory tape replayed that tragic experience as if it were a scene from the movie *Groundhog Day* which had the character reliving the same day of his life over and over again. But there was no humor, no Bill Murray, and no Andie MacDowell in my private movie. Instead, there were clips of a rhythmic upper body rocking and the sudden appearance of blood in a peaceful ear canal. There was the gradual recognition of rescuers and the group energy focusing on attempting to save one life, then gradually accepting we could not do enough. It was time, time for his spirit to vacate his body.

I've wondered since, *"Would I handle dying the same way today?"* I don't know. Working with death was an experience that made me stronger. It also made me weaker. With this "10-40" under my belt I had a new yardstick to measure and compare future fatalities. If I could handle that one, then I could handle the next one. But somewhere in my subconscious the death had taken its toll. My career calling, being a deputy, still had its fun times and rewarding moments, but I would never be the same. For the first time, I had watched a person die.

The wreck on Yoder Road, seven-tenths of a mile south of US 50, is a story I still summarize to many an older student when we discuss the dangers of drinking and driving. I'll tell my audience about that young couple who were careful enough to not drink and drive so that they could have a safe honeymoon. I'll tell them that the the engaged woman had been both married and widowed in the same evening. The culprit interfering with these life plans was a teenage boy who just wanted to have a good time drinking beer, not intending to harm anyone. Yet, his decision altered many people's lives, including his own.

When I'm leading a class in school and we're discussing substance abuse we consider those survivors. How were they affected? I hear about the concerns for the widow, the parents of the groom, other family members and friends, even unborn generations. Often, I'll point out to the students that the witnesses, EMTs, fire personnel and police officers present were also, to some degree, traumatized, if not victimized. The memory causes me to swallow deeply. When I recall the event for a group, I do so in the hope that the one death and one criminal conviction, twenty-five years ago, may help prevent additional heartache today and tomorrow. This is my way of giving life to the dead and injured, and a plea for drinkers to not drive.

The fatality victim lives on today. I remember him and I continue to tell my students about his last few dying minutes on this earthly plain. Like parents who erect crosses on the road or create scholarships in the name of their child, I want his death to be remembered and to make a difference. *It does!* I see it often when students write an essay for my class, they recall the concrete, not abstract, heart-stopping consequences of drinking and driving.

I'm asked what happened to the drunk driver. I almost apologize. Since he had no criminal record, with his guilty plea the courts gave him probation—no jail time.

Because of the carnage on the road due to drunk drivers like him, our country did enact new laws with stiffer penalties. I never inquired as to any civil suits. I was never subpoenaed for a trial. To my knowledge, I never had further contact with the injured, convicted driver or the surviving, widowed passenger. I've wondered about them though. We shared a moment in time. I hope both are doing fine and making a positive difference in our world. And always, I feel regret for the families.

7

ETHICAL ENCOUNTERS

"DID YOU KNOW ANY POLICE OFFICERS WHEN YOU WERE OUR AGE?"

> *"Injustice anywhere is a threat to justice everywhere."*
> —Martin Luther King Jr.[9]

"438, Dispatch."
"Go ahead, 438."
"10-6 traffic on K-61 at Bone Springs Road with Kansas R-Robert, E-Edward, D-David, 1-0-1."
"10-4, 438."

Within two minutes of the radio broadcast I slowly drive by the traffic stop. I take a quick look at the dark green van whose driver is leaning intently into his side-view mirror. In the front passenger seat is a child. The marked patrol unit, with its rotating red and blue lights, is stopped about twenty feet to the rear of the likely speeder. I can see the deputy behind the wheel of her cruiser, already writing a ticket while continuing to observe the van. She notices me as well. In a split second we make eye contact. My hands on the steering wheel, I give a partial wave or salute with the tightened ends of my fingers of my left hand. In turn, the traffic officer conserves even more energy. She gives me an almost imperceptible, miniscule, but meaningful nod, answering my question, telling me the only thing I need to know. "No problem. I'm okay." So I continue in route to my school assignment.

Soon I'll be in front of a class of nearly twenty fourth grade students wanting to know from me what it's like being a police officer. Where do I begin to explain? I prepare myself by thinking back to when I was growing up as a ten-year old. What did I know about police officers? Where had I received most of my information? I had a next door neighbor who was a police officer, but he certainly wasn't an influence in my career choice. Even though we were neighbors, the truth is, he was as rare a sight as a cool breeze during a Kansas wheat harvest. He was seemingly always out of the picture, gone, working or sleeping. My only glimpse of him was on the sidewalk between the front door of his house and his personal automobile. Since I didn't really know him, the few stories I had heard about his work were secondhand via his children, my playmates.

As with today's youth, a lot of the information I knew about law enforcement came from sitting about six feet in front of a television set. Only in my childhood most of the seasonal programs were of marshals and sheriffs, wearing their white hats, chasing the bad guys from atop a four-legged stallion, not from behind a horse-powered Mustang or Bronco. Back then, if asked, "What do deputies do?" I would have answered with the knowledge I had gleaned from the perspective of a viewer of Saturday morning entertainment, packaged in nearly identical half-hour scripts.

Deputies chased people who broke the law, used their keen tracking abilities, made an arrest after a physical struggle, and brought the mean, if not evil, criminal to jail. The criminal offense might have been stealing horses, robbing banks or murdering innocent settlers. And the setting for the shows? Within each weekly western episode was a community of white people in the midst of physically harsh surroundings, sometimes the victims of menacing Indians "on the warpath." One ever-present theme was that when bad men chose to do bad things it was up to courageous lawmen to right the wrong. These were real lawmen to me, not actors. I viewed them as the thin, gray line between anarchy and peace, not staged images between commercials. *"Could I ever be so daring?"* I wondered. If I could be like them then I had the potential to help make the world a safer place to live.

Gradually the plug was pulled on weekly western television shows, replaced by more modern cops and robbers. But I had certainly been influenced in my formative years by exposure to a predictable formula where western lawmen were always right, and after seemingly insurmountable struggles always got their man.

Later in life after a short time on the department as a deputy, I knew from first hand experience that I'd been wrong about a few things. Law "men" are not always right and they don't always get their suspect. But I was acutely aware that officers (men and women) on a daily basis put their lives on the line in order to help maintain law and order in our society. Whether it's a traffic stop, an undercover buy, a search warrant or a domestic violence call, officers die doing their job. They also pay an incredible price because of the stress of their work.

Another exposure I had to police officers as a child was on our summer vacations when my father would attempt to get as many miles away from home as early and quickly as possible. Too often Dad, who was in a hurry, was caught speeding. That was my early training on traffic stops from the point of view of a youngster in the back seat. It furthered my education about enforcing the law in that I knew the ticket was justified; we were speeding. I also knew that Dad was a good person. This taught me that people could get into trouble for their actions without a debate about their character. It was always a monetary fine and never, thank goodness, a trip to jail. It was on those vacations that I got to see up close the process of Dad taking risks, trying to avoid being detected, and then being upset at himself and sometimes the officer when the traffic cop did his job. He caught us.

Our family vacations were sometimes slowed by serious car wrecks where beside the twisted vehicles a person's lifeless body was lying on the ground with a blanket covering at least the face. I remember being pressed to the backseat's side window, knowing I only had a few seconds to attempt to figure out what had happened at the fatality scene. I wondered what it felt like to be one of those officers working the accident, to be involved in something so final. And I remember always saying a prayer for the recently departed, the family, and for our safe arrival at our destination that night. Years later, when I became an officer and was the one working the fatality wreck I was still saying prayers for the departing souls. I'd also catch the occasional eye of a child staring out at the scene from a passing vehicle, trying to make sense of the mangled wreckage.

While growing up I didn't have a three-dimensional, live, police officer as a friend or role model. But Boy Scouts prepared me to serve in uniform. It reinforced the values I believed were important—to be a good person. The Scout law, oath (or promise), motto and slogan all connected with me. I aimed to be that ideal Scout, to "be prepared" for anything and to "do a good turn daily."[10] Scouts also reinforced a message I received at home and at church: faith in God and country.

The Scout law gave me twelve character traits to hold up as personal goals for me to examine and to challenge myself with and to improve upon daily. These traits were my memorized check list that I used to evaluate myself. Often as a child, when I would say my nightly prayers I used the Scout law as a moral compass. In fact, I knew the twelve points of the Scout law better than the Bible's ten commandments.

When I attended the law enforcement academy a few months after being hired as a deputy sheriff, I was introduced to our profession's code of ethics. Like the Scout oath it was a clear reminder of the great responsibilities each of us was accepting as individuals, even though it focused on us as public officials. The code continues to be a guiding light, a measuring stick of my personal and professional success and failure.

Law enforcement code of ethics:

> *As a law enforcement officer, my*
> *fundamental duty is to serve*
> *mankind; to safeguard lives and*
> *property; to protect the innocent*
> *against deception, the weak against*
> *oppression or intimidation, and*
> *the peaceful against violence or*
> *disorder; and to respect the*
> *Constitutional rights of all men*
> *to liberty, equality and justice.*
>
> *...Honest in thought and deed in*
> *both my personal and official life,*
> *I will be exemplary in obeying the*
> *laws of the land and the regulations*
> *of my department.*[11]

Today I carry a card in my wallet that I share with some of my classes when we are talking about doing the right thing. My printed reminder tells me to "Never compromise your integrity!" and then lists eight questions on its "ethical dilemma test."[12]

They are:
1. Am I acting out of anger, lust, peer pressure or greed?
2. Is my decision legal?
3. Would I do it if my family were standing beside me?
4. How will it make me feel in twenty years?
5. Is it worth my job and career?
6. What would I do if I were being video taped?
7. Would my loved ones be proud or ashamed?
8. Am I following the Golden Rule?[13]

The mention of the Golden Rule on my ethical dilemma test card brings me full circle. It is where I began and it's who I am: to treat others as you would have them treat you. This is what I was taught as a child, as a scout and in my career in law enforcement.

8

NATIONAL SECURITY

"WHEN DID YOU KNOW YOU WANTED TO BE A POLICE OFFICER?"

"If you do the crime you got to do the time."
—common saying in prison

My great-grandfather was a Nickerson, Kansas blacksmith and city marshal. His son, my grandfather, was also a city marshal (and ran the town's road grader) for South Hutchinson, Kansas. My dad was a soldier in the European theater during World War II. These family ties and my daily dose of western TV shows as a child, influenced me at an early age to picture myself working in the field of criminal justice. But as an adult I never seriously considered that any form of law enforcement called me until I became a part-time security officer working at a store in Carbondale, Illinois. Jokingly, I would tell my friends, "I work for National Security." It was true, but the badge in my wallet said "Security," while my work environment was in a regional grocery store chain called "National."

I was soon surprised by how quickly catching shoplifters got in my blood. It was invigorating! Having never hunted, this activity truly raised my heart beat and challenged my senses in the same way. *"Did he really just put that can inside his backpack?" "Did I just see what I thought I did?"* I threw away any stereotypes I might have had as to who shoplifts. Who shoplifts? Not everyone, but anyone! Every shopper became a potential criminal when I was on duty. Dressed in plain clothes, I would push a shopping cart around the store, picking up out of place items, all the while checking out the shopping habits of the public.

The job, the hunt, taught me to be observant and stealthy. If I saw a lady with an empty, but huge purse, I was alert. If the temperature outside was mild but the shopper wore a heavy coat, I wondered why. Mostly I learned to watch people's mannerisms and body language. Why did they have to keep looking over their shoulder to decide what to buy? And were shoppers signaling one another? I learned to be aware of my peripheral vision when I focused solely on one person. *My* mannerisms, in following a suspected shoplifter could easily be detected when viewed by a second suspect causing the potential crime to be postponed to another time or place.

A college student would take an apple and yogurt by putting them in her purse. An off duty security guard, after a look over his shoulder, would pocket canned tuna fish to his jacket. Teenagers and adults would attempt the theft of a whole carton of cigarettes by sticking the box up their shirt or holding it in their armpit under their jacket. Kids would steal candy. A wealthy pregnant shopper was caught with a purse full of greeting cards. *"Was this part of her lifestyle prior to her pregnancy,"* I wondered, *"or due to her temporary condition?"* As she headed out the door at home did she tell her husband, "I'm going out for ice cream, pickles, and greeting cards," knowing she was going to steal something or was it an impulsive act?

The part-time, stimulating store activity made for great story telling at my full-time teaching job. I would tell the inquisitive students how stealing wasn't usually about being poor. Most of the customers we caught would ask two questions: "Can I pay for it now?" and, after we informed them of the seriousness of their offense, "Do you have to call the police?" In nearly all of my apprehensions the offender had enough cash to pay for the items they attempted to steal. I didn't know the extent of anyone's larger economic problems, just whether they had money in their wallet.

Looking back now, I missed a real opportunity of discussing with the youth at school the ever-present fact of economic inequalities in our world. People who are desperate—with limited resources—make choices that are often not understood by people that have economic stability. Those like me, who take for granted that they will have enough to eat, find it remarkably easy to judge others who are poor and hungry. While congratulating myself on my wealth I often forget the influence of my parents who helped create opportunities for my success. Put another way, "Some people are born on third base and go through life thinking they hit a triple."[14]

I remember the young man I hadn't suspected of doing anything, who was slowly pushing his nearly empty shopping cart around the store. Among his few gathered items, I noticed that two were expensive steaks and wondered if they were worth watching. At the end of the aisle the shopper walked out of my view, but I was aware that the cart's wheels hesitated for a brief moment. When I passed by, visually checking his packaged food, I realized the steaks were gone! I couldn't believe it! He was *fast!* Backtracking, my eyes frantically searching the shelves, I found no steaks—only non-perishables in their rows of conformity. My heart, with its pounding pulse, my unblinking eyes and my adrenaline-charged brain were all on high alert. I backed off and let the special customer buy his inexpensive groceries, then meander out the store's front door.

Just outside, after identifying myself as security and asking him to return with me, his pleading began. "I'm on parole and if I get into any more trouble I'll have to go back to prison. Please, give me a break! Don't do this to me! I'll never do it again." While I wanted to immediately lecture him, I followed the security rules. I didn't get into an explanation of the offender's possible consequences until we were safely in the back room of the store, management had been notified, and we had learned the identification of the alleged thief.

My answer to the stealer of steaks and others who shopped for free was matter of fact and seemingly uncaring. "When you shoplifted it was your choice. Now there are consequences for that action. I didn't take the merchandise.

You did." Then I'd ask him and others that followed to cooperate so that their penalty didn't get any worse. Usually everyone I caught yielded to my authority. But I remember three cases that became more stimulating than I had ever expected once I left the relative safety of the store. To this day I recall the individuals as characters: Lamb Chop, Mountain Man and Bruce Lee.

Case #1. One night I followed a slimly built college-age student out of the store after he had shoplifted an item from the meat counter. After identifying myself he took off, sprinting across the parking lot. I realized I was on my own. I hadn't had the opportunity, as I usually did, to alert management to my suspected shoplifter. He was determined not to be caught, but I was in an equally focused frame of mind. I wanted him and I was confident I would get him. Being a runner, my plan was to let him keep a safe distance ahead while wearing him out. Along the way, though, the further we got away from the store, the more I began to wonder how I was going to bring him back if he became a struggling subject. Then, as he ran by the rear of a business I saw him reaching inside his jacket and belt.

I slowed, hoping it wasn't a weapon. I was pleased to observe him with one quick underhanded stroke fling a wrapped lamb chop onto the roof of a nearby building. Soon, he slowed and stopped. Out of breath, he turned to me and said, "I didn't take anything." As I kept my hand on his belt and had him hand me his driver's license, I was pleasantly surprised to see a National grocery store employee approach us and ask me if I needed assistance. I told him to check the roof of the business where our fleeing customer had thrown a package of meat. Minutes later the three of us and the retrieved lamb chop returned to the store where the police were called.

When the offender was unwilling to admit his guilt to the police I knew that the alleged theft might be more likely to wind up in court. Besides detailed paperwork documenting the circumstances of the case, I made sure to hold on to that lamb chop. It was evidence. The store let me secure it in my own refrigerator at my apartment. Six months later, after a couple of legal court continuances on the last day before the college's summer vacation began, I appeared in court with my subpoena in one hand and the bagged lamb chop in the other. The alleged thief and his lawyer were present, but seeing me silently (and purposefully) inspecting the still frozen evidence wrapped in white butcher paper, led them to plead to the criminal offense.

Before ever becoming a deputy sheriff I had received a valuable lesson, that no matter how good an arrest or apprehension, without the evidence and one's presence in court, the initial work was wasted effort. You had to be prepared to go the distance, whether running down the suspect, taking the time to do the investigation correctly, or adapting to the snail's pace of the criminal justice system.

Case #2. As just illustrated, not everyone was willing to cooperate with unarmed security personnel. This was especially true if the suspect was a whole lot bigger and stronger. In this particular incident I've forgotten what was stolen, but I remember the mammoth size of the shoplifter I confronted. I still recall thinking that there was no way I was going outside by myself without notifying management, because I'd be needing someone to call the ambulance for me! I even requested that Big Oscar, the butcher, assist us.

When our suspect walked out the door he drew a crowd of employees. I made my standard request for cooperation. Surrounded, against the side of the building, the cornered customer lunged and kicked off the wall with one leg in an attempt to flee, launching himself towards us like a Civil War cannon ball at a low trajectory. Suddenly, after his leap we were all on him grabbing body parts. Despite his size and good lungs, four of us quickly had him horizontally in tow. I felt like I was helping deliver rolled up carpet! I can still see the customers in their check-out lines, eyeing us as we carried this struggling patron unceremoniously to the rear office for internal processing. I would wager that all the bug-eyed customers and would-be shoplifters eagerly *paid* for their groceries that day. We were not ordinary grocery store workers. We were National Security!

Once in the store's back office it took awhile for everyone to settle down from the excitement. Our prisoner who was in a windowless room with us blocking the only door, had apparently lost his fight. He became quiet and noncombative and my muscle-bound carpet carrying team gradually filtered back to their full-time duties. It was then, after a couple of minutes of regaining my composure and beginning the paperwork that I had an uncomfortable feeling that something wasn't right. I recognized the silence.

No one was talking or even breathing deeply. Where was Bob? Where was Oscar? It was at that moment that my nearby mountain of a man grabbed a loose lock and chain from atop a nearby employee's parked bicycle, swung it backwards and screamed, "I'm getting out of here!" We were in close quarters and I instinctively grabbed his arm. The two of us struggled and we immediately went to the floor. Time slowed and I remember thinking in long, complete thoughts. One was, *"I'm doing pretty good, he's got to have a hundred pounds on me!"* followed by, *"I hope the police get here soon!"* and then, more urgently, *"I hope they were called, he's a lot stronger than I am!"*

I had prematurely congratulated myself three times: first, for being alert to the attempted theft; second, on the group apprehension; and then third, on my competitive wrestling skills with this mass of sumo-like dimensions. But while I had relaxed, assuming the riskiest part of our encounter was over, my prisoner had watched and waited until the conditions favored his escape. I had absolutely let my guard down and he took advantage.

As we skirmished on the tile floor, tied up like two twisted pretzels fighting for freedom, unable to recognize our own limbs, Mountain Man began gouging both my eyes with his thumbs! I wasn't doing as well as I had at first surmised. Then, unintentionally, one of his pinky fingers entered my gasping mouth. Time stopped for me. I recalled how my mom had always told my sister, Mary, and me, "Fight fairly!" when, in our pre-teen days we battled daily. She wasn't worried about a knife fight or the use of other weapons of mass destruction. Mom just didn't want me to hit Mary too high in the chest and she didn't want Mary to kick me in the groin.

But that nanosecond memory of parental instruction in the home, in regard to a family fight, was now hurting my chances of survival in the real world. This struggling stranger just didn't seem to know or care about my mother's middle class rules. In the heat of the moment I rejected her squarely civilized model of manners! My brain, in a flash, assured me that biting was an appropriate response under these trying circumstances. I had sorted things out. I bit, thought, then bit harder! He started yelling and as he was getting up, I knew I wasn't done with him.

For the first time in my life I had reached my savage or survival mode! But before I could further test my new junkyard dog persona, my untapped reservoir of adrenalin, my opponent pushed open the swinging doors only to discover two police officers slowly approaching. They had arrived to take a report and make an arrest in what they had been told was a controlled situation.

My childhood memories of western TV shows again came alive. I was in the Longbranch Saloon in *Gunsmoke*, a weekly television series. At the climax of the show there was often a scene that took the viewer from the saloon to the streets for a grand finale shootout. But before exiting to the town's main street, Marshal Dillon would look outside for his challenger then lightly push through the swinging doors.

As Mountain Man began to leave I again heard those same creaking sounds of the swinging doors from *Gunsmoke,* only this time the good guys were approaching from the other side. I celebrated. *"Yes! The cavalry has arrived!"* Marshal Matt Dillon and his sidekick Chester had returned for an encore in my adult life. My prayers were answered, and Mountain Man gave up again, this time peacefully. But that day, unlike in my TV memories, there was no shootout. Instead, the police officers made an arrest without incident. My challenger left in handcuffs.

After the officers hauled off the submissive batterer I reflected on what had happened. First off, where did all my help go? This had *not* been a typical apprehension, so we should have been more cautious until the police arrived. Secondly, why on earth did we have a bicycle lock and chain lying around for any apprehended shoplifter to use as a weapon if he chose to be violent? And lastly, as I thought about the way I handled myself, including the biting, I smiled at how it's sometimes necessary to one's survival to use all available resources. Fighting "fairly" works best between siblings and friends, not between desperate, skinny security men trying to prevent the escape of cornered criminals.

Later in my shift, one of the officers returned for additional information and to see if I wanted to press battery charges. He advised me that one reason the suspect had wanted to "rabbit" before the police arrived was that there was an active arrest warrant for him. Before I could ask him if it was for attempted murder he told me it was a possession of marijuana charge.

Similar incidents regularly occur in the world of law enforcement. A traffic stop is made for a minor violation and the officer is injured or killed. Why? Because sometimes the officer may assume that because the violation is only an infraction, not an arrestable offense, that the driver should see it from a similar perspective. But *"just* a warning" or *"just* a ticket" in the eyes of an officer may be interpreted much differently by the driver, especially if he or she has just committed a felony offense, is wanted for prior violations, or is high on mind-altering drugs. Some people will take *any* necessary action to keep from going to jail or prison, depending on their beliefs, mood, mental state, and, or, experience. Mountain Man saw that sticking around, waiting for the police, and going to jail as more painful than fighting his way out of the store. It was an easy choice for him. In the past, fighting had most likely helped him get what he wanted.

Case #3. I vividly recall this last incident due to how it affected me emotionally. This time I was scared! It began when I caught a female shoplifter who was probably encouraged, if not instructed in the theft by her boyfriend. He was shopping with her in the store. I didn't believe I had enough proof that he was directly involved, so she was the only one apprehended and processed by us and the police. Months later the boyfriend was back but with another friend. He hadn't seen me in the store, but I recognized him, so I remained hidden from view behind a two-way mirror. I thought to myself, *"Maybe I can catch him this time."*

Soon, my one-time acquaintance was walking around the store eating a pair of sugary cupcakes. Since he was still shopping I figured he hadn't taken the time to return to the front of the store to pay the cashier. I also doubted he'd bring the empty package to the counter upon checking out, in order to be accountable for the food item. So I watched and waited.

When he and his male friend prepared to leave I quickly located the cupcake wrapper sitting on a rear fruit counter, not hidden, but out in the open. Immediately, I chose to interpret his placement of that wrapper as a calling card: *"I was here and you didn't catch me."* For some reason I was taking this one personally, but why? Did I see him as the instigator of the earlier theft that got away without any legal consequences? Maybe I blamed myself for not having a better case or for not trying harder to link him to the crime. I clearly viewed him as cocky and arrogant to walk around *our* store and openly eat his way to the check-out lane. Did he think he was immune from following the rules set by society? Apparently so. It was time he had a wake up call.

As my target and his acquaintance left the store, I quickly double-checked with the cashier to be sure they hadn't paid for the digesting sweets. My frame of mind was not clear or calm when I followed him outside towards their car. I approached him preoccupied. He recognized me. I displayed his abandoned cupcake wrapper and sarcastically challenged him, "I think you forgot to pay for this." He instantly, intensely, was ready for battle. In one movement he kicked off his thongs (sandals, not a skimpy swim suit bottom), pulled up his loose pant legs, and crouched into a stance of readiness.

He wasn't Asian, but in his actions he resembled martial art expert Bruce Lee! I felt overwhelmed! Where was my confidence now? Yelling at me, he told me how I had cost him his girlfriend and that I would pay for it! As customers and store employees became spectators under the artificial lamp post lights, we were actors on a stage. He promised me that he knew what I looked like and he'd find me to settle up. The store manager worked to calm things down. My challenger and his friend quickly agreed to leave the parking lot, but as my martial art suspect was driven away he had the last word. With his pointed index finger punctuating the still night air he exclaimed, "I'll get you!" I said nothing as I carefully, calmly, copied down the speeding car's license tag number, watching it disappear into nothingness.

But I was shaken. Never had my job seemed so dangerous. I had known intellectually the risks of confronting strangers outside the store. I was aware that people sometimes carry guns. This was different. This had become personal. When his crazed eyes looked into mine, I felt their intensity. He meant business and I took him seriously. Before I left in my car that night I meticulously scanned the parking area and beyond. I wasn't afraid of my own shadow, but I was looking for his. Was he watching me? Would I be followed? Was the prey now the hunter? *"So, this is how it feels to be tracked!"* I thought. It was no longer fun. Now it was *my* safety, *my* life! As I drove into the night, taking a circuitous route home, I checked my rear-view mirror, checked it again, looking for him, not recognizing myself.

I never saw my Bruce Lee challenger again, but I learned how my idealism for world peace sure didn't hold up under a single, serious personal threat. After returning home the night of the assault I called the police to see what legal options I had in order to better defend myself if confronted in the future. I even asked about purchasing and carrying a gun! Fear can sure be a motivator to change.

I never bought a weapon for protection. Within a couple of days my anxiety passed, but the whole experience was a lesson for future reference. I had learned firsthand how a domestic violence victim could be scared to inaction *or* action. Having felt this raw emotion, it was now much more clear to me how kids could see a weapon as a necessity for their personal protection from harassment or bodily harm. If I, with all my resources, so quickly jumped at the idea of getting a gun, then what about the younger, weaker person without a support system, the one who felt alone and helpless? What about those people with physical or mental disabilities, those who spoke a language different from the majority in a community, or those who were foreign to a community's culture? Anyone who felt like an outsider, felt they were disenfranchised or a potential victim could also easily decide to take the law into their own hands for one reason: their self-preservation.

How long had I been living in my ivory tower? Forever! As an early teen I'd been in a couple of fights, and lost, but mostly my exposure to violence had been limited to news accounts in the media. Fortunately, I had grown up in a peaceful community environment. So many others didn't have that luxury. My parking lot encounter forced me to become emotionally involved in looking for options to violence. How could so many potentially aggressive encounters be more reasonably avoided? There had to be workable answers. This became a quest for me and remains so today as I continue to search for alternatives to violence. One perspective I have is that in our culture, violence is too often seen as a solution to the problem rather than a symptom of the many ills of our society.

9

Keep A Sense of Humor

"WHAT'S THE FUNNIEST THING THAT'S EVER HAPPENED TO YOU ON DUTY?"

"425, Dispatch."
"425, Go ahead."
"425, Dispatch. I'm in the parking lot at Dillons, 5th & Adams. Request a PD unit with a lock-out tool 10-43 me here. There's a child locked in the vehicle with the windows rolled up."
"10-4, 425."

Years ago in a grocery store parking lot, on a hot and humid day, an agitated citizen stopped an officer, reporting a baby in need of help. The Good Samaritan had seen the baby in the back of a locked car with no one around.

The veteran sheriff's deputy was soon glaring into the tightly sealed vehicle. His hurried observation revealed a sleeping baby, secured in an infant seat, with a pink blanket partially covering her head. Only later would he bluntly describe her in two words: "butt ugly."

Promptly the officer radioed dispatch requesting a city officer respond with a special tool to unlock the car. But calling for help was his undoing, for this officer had a reputation far and wide for practical jokes on unsuspecting citizens and deputies. This one moment would forever alter, yet cement, his reputation of prank behavior.

Ironically, he, of all officers didn't need help in opening locked cars. He was an expert at it from years of experience, especially when the vehicles were patrol units. How many times had a tired officer, just starting his shift, turned his cruiser's ignition key on in the semi-darkness of the law enforcement parking lot, only to be jolted erect due to a shrieking siren, blaring radios, aggressive windshield wipers and a whirl of emergency lights? In survival mode, the frantic officer would grapple for knobs and switches to turn off.

Back at the grocery store parking lot a PD officer soon arrived, exited her unit, and through the window checked on the unconscious, lifeless body. With a "Gotcha!" in her authoritative voice, she announced to dispatch and all listening officers that she had miraculously completed her assignment and was ready for another. "10-24, 10-8, no case," she announced. "This is *not* a baby. It's a Cabbage Patch doll!"

And to this day, at least in local law enforcement circles, a Cabbage Patch doll, popular in the mid-1980s, is forever synonymous with one retired, now deceased, practical joker who finally had his "comeuppance."

* * *

It's another day. I'm in a sixth grade classroom teaching D.A.R.E.® (Drug Abuse Resistance Education) as we start the class by using the question box. I unfold the paper and read: "Sgt. Potter, what's the funniest thing that's ever happened to you on your job?"

I smile, then frown.

As a new patrol officer I wanted to prove to my sergeants and myself that I could do the job. On second shift one afternoon near dusk I was assigned to an abandoned vehicle, a Chevy pickup, which had been parked on the edge of the paved road for three days. Dispatch also advised me that a dog was in the cab of the pickup. As I pulled up, my sergeant informed me by radio that he was familiar with the hazard and I should have the vehicle towed.

Parking directly behind the truck, I exited my patrol car to see if the doors were locked. As I walked up to the side of the pickup's bed, grasping its side, I was nearly scared out of my body armor as a white German shepherd lunged toward me from the open rear window! He had timed his growl at the peak of his leap and for a split second I was *frozen*! I hadn't noticed that the rear window was missing its glass. This was great officer training. I had been caught off guard and yet, somehow survived. Fortunately for me the dog retreated back into his lair.

I knew the dog was just doing his duty, protecting his master's property, but I wondered why the canine had been left behind. Was it to guard this old pickup from someone stealing parts? Then I reminded myself that this aged pickup might be someone's only means of transportation. But, where was the owner? Dispatch had been unable to reach the registered title-holder who had reportedly moved to an unknown address. The vehicle, with its tires touching the edge of the road, parked on a hill, was a traffic hazard and a liability to our department if it wasn't moved.

Following orders, I was *determined* to find a way to have this pickup removed. But first I would have to engage the solitary sentry before I could disengage the emergency brake. With a plan in mind I requested dispatch to contact the towing service and to ask them to bring some steak bones along in order to help clear the cab of this canine.

When the tow-truck driver arrived he granted my wish, carrying dog bones in a dish. He and I tried to coax and bribe the dog from its home away from home but to no avail. From the driver's partially open door I then poked my baton at the dog with the passenger-side door wide open. It was an invitation to avoid my police harassment. But as evidence of his refusal he growled and contributed bite marks to my wooden nightstick. Then, suddenly, he had a change of heart and jumped out the door to the ground.

Would he attack us or run off? Instead of being aggressive he surrendered. He ran around to the back of the pickup to the driver's side of my patrol car and jumped in through my open window! With one more graceful hop he was in the back seat, tongue and tail wagging, ready for a Sunday drive in the country in my marked patrol unit!

I should have had a belly laugh. Instead, I grimaced and weakly smiled. The pickup was free to tow. I had completed my mission.

However, man's best friend occupied my patrol car and our department didn't have a K-9 unit. I wasn't ready to start one. For another second I considered the alternatives. There were no county animal control officers. If I drove the dog to the city's animal shelter without a muzzle he could attack me from behind more viciously than any handcuffed prisoner. My patrol unit had no rear seat cage, which might have allowed me to transport the critter. Despite his apparent willingness to get along, I couldn't count on him remaining calm.

When I opened the patrol car's back door and my visitor jumped out and eagerly took off across a field, I felt relief and gratitude in the ease of recapturing my vehicle. I regretted I didn't have a better solution. The canine, who was just doing his personal best for his absent owner, deserved better.

* * *

When you encourage kids to publicly share, you will guarantee some embarrassing moments. I recall one from years ago. I was visiting the younger grades, using chart paper in my presentation. One large piece was set up on an easel at a height the children could reach. The paper had a human figure outline on it that I had previously drawn, representing a police officer. Bold colored markers were nearby for selection and use by the children.

I explained to the class that I would choose

volunteers one at a time to come up to the front of the class. There they would draw a piece of equipment on the officer using a marker of their choice. Then I'd ask the artist-speaker to tell the class what they drew (in case I didn't recognize it). Finally, I'd talk for a few moments about the piece of equipment before we moved on to the next volunteer. It was a good plan because it involved the children actively doing, not just listening. The class learned about the parts of my uniform.

Before I had completed my instructions hands shot up in the air. Plenty of willing volunteers were eager to participate. They knew about drawing and they were able to observe my uniform and equipment. This was guaranteed success! After selecting a boy to draw, he proudly showed off a huge, bold star as the first contribution to the evolving class project.

"And what is that?" I inquired.

"A badge," he replied.

"Good job! We have a real artist here. Yes, the officer's badge helps people understand who is a police officer. But you know if I lost my badge and you found it, would that make you a police officer?" I got them thinking.

"No," a half dozen scattered voices responded, along with a couple of softer "Yes" votes. Others still pondered the question.

"We wouldn't be a *real* police officer," a student explained.

"Is your badge made of real gold?" asked a student from the back of the classroom.

"No," was my short answer, but I smiled thinking of my own childhood when I thought badges could stop bullets. Later, I passed the gold-plated, tin metal badge around and the children felt its lightness. Since I already carried an extra fourteen pounds of equipment every time I dressed for work, I didn't mind something lighter than it looked.

"Who's next?" I continued. A girl was called on who drew a more recognizable helmet than my own stunted artistic skills allowed. She identified the piece of equipment, was commended, and I asked the class why an officer might need a helmet. For a few moments we discussed car crashes, motorcycle helmets, and being protected from "bad guys" who would hit officers on the head.

I started thinking that the interaction was really going well when a boy volunteered, came up front and drew two good sized, horizontally connected circles several inches below the waist, right in the mid-groin area of the outlined officer!

Suddenly, I realized I was out of my comfort zone. I looked for help. Where was the teacher? She was in the back of the room sitting at her desk with her head facing downwards, her forehead held in the palm of one hand, the elbow resting on the desk. Her head was slowly moving sideways, left, then right, then left. Was she laughing or crying? I couldn't tell. She was unable or unwilling to look at me. No teacher to the rescue so I reminded myself, *"I'm in charge."* Then, as insurance, I crossed my fingers, trusting that it would work out, and said to the little boy, "Very good! And tell us what you have drawn...."

"Handcuffs" was his immediate, innocent and proud reply.

With a sigh of relief and a big smile I thanked him. I was again grateful. Not one student had apparently noticed any similarity between the two huge circles and that of the male anatomy. I took my handcuffs from my belt case and told the class how they were used when we made arrests and took people to jail. I was back in charge. I had dodged another imaginary bullet. I was becoming a seasoned veteran in the classroom. The lesson I learned was to trust that everything will turn out okay and when I'm puzzled with a student's response, to remember to ask the children what something means to them. I also reminded myself to keep a sense of humor.

10

K-9s (Canines)

"WHERE'S MY TOY?"

Official: *Ladies and gentlemen, we are gathered here today to honor Adam, the sheriff's department's K-9 and his handler Deputy...*

Adam: *"Where's my toy?"*

Official: *...their fight against drugs makes our community safer...*

Adam: *"Where's my toy?"*

Official: *...for their teamwork and dedication we present this engraved plaque which reads...*

Adam: *"That's not my toy! Where's my toy?"*

Anyone with a dog has many, many stories to tell. One of the first lessons I learned visiting grade school classrooms was that one unconscious reference to a dog could sabotage the entire lesson plan. I never saw any students drooling, but casually mentioning the word "dog" seemed to signal some Pavlovian conditioned reflex, causing the children to uncontrollably bark out comments about their own family pet. On the other hand, I've also seen how these same students, once they reach middle school, are much less likely to spontaneously ramble on with personal narratives about man's best friend.

In one small seventh grade class I visited regularly we had been discussing the effects and consequences of tobacco, alcohol, marijuana and methamphetamine. As a follow up we invited our department's canine (K-9) handler to bring his drug detecting dog into the classroom as a show-and-tell visitor. I knew he would be well received, especially after learning that all the students but one had a pet dog at home. This was clearly a dog friendly group.

Our K-9 handler had learned a thing or two about presentations before ever stepping into our classroom. He knew that if he were going to hold the audience's attention he would have to keep the four-legged, tongue-wagging, hyperactive, charismatic star off center stage until late in the show. This was an officer with public speaking savvy.

* * *

"Good morning class!" I welcome the students. "As promised we have our department's K-9 officer here today. Please help me welcome Deputy Charles Collins."

Clap, clap, clap.

"Now, I'd like each of you to introduce yourself to Deputy Collins in this manner. Say your first name, and if you have a dog, tell us its breed and then its name."

"My name is Carly. I have a mini dachshund named Taffy."

"My name is Tyler. We have a collie named Rocky."

"My name is Amanda and my family has a schnauzer we call Sammie."

"I'm Tiffany. I have a miniature Yorkshire terrier named Samson and a miniature longhaired dachshund who answers to Brandy."

"Hi. My name's Sarah and my mini shelty is Zoe."

"I'm Elizabeth. We don't have a dog, but I know it's weird, we have eight cats. Their names are Smokey, Kitty, Sassy, Shadow, Lucky, Princess, Boots and Ugly."

"My name is Raven. We have a retriever by the name of Simba and a pit bull named O.J."

"My name's Cody. My dog's name is Duke and I don't know what kind of dog he is."

"I'm Trevor. My dog, Zeke, is a mixture of Lab and malamute."

"My name is Kristin and our dog is a Lab mix named Oreo."

"Hello. My name's Brooke. We have three dogs of unknown breeds. They are Charlie, Daisy and Dakota."

"Thank you very much for those introductions!" I respond enthusiastically. "I didn't know there were so many dogs out there! Elizabeth, we've got cats, not dogs, at our house too. Their names are Butch, a Manx; Hoover, a Siamese; Gray, a Russian blue, and Home Boy or Homes, a tabby.

"It's time now to have Officer Collins tell us about his dog. Are you ready to listen to Officer Collins?"

"Yes!" the class eagerly responds.

"Deputy Collins! Take it from here...."

"Like the Sarge says, the Sheriff's Department has a dog, a Belgian Malinois, named Adam. He's two-and-a-half years old and has been helping us out for the last six months. He was born in Europe. His job is to find hidden drugs.

"Adam has already notched several canine assists where he discovered illegal drugs or drug paraphernalia while checking out cars that other officers have stopped. He's also been involved in searches of houses when there's been a search warrant obtained.

"When Adam is requested at the scene of a stopped vehicle it's because of suspicious circumstances. Once we arrive I lead him around the vehicle and he smells the air outside the car. Doing this is not a violation of a person's rights. If Adam determines drugs are nearby, he alerts. That means he will paw at the place where he smells an odor. When he shows me, the handler, that he smells the scent of drugs then there's a reason for a search warrant. Usually, despite the strong possibility that drugs will be discovered and the driver arrested, the suspect consents to allow the officers to search the car.

"Some of you may wonder how drug dogs are selected..."

"Pardon me, Officer Collins," I interrupt, "If drivers know there are drugs hidden in the car then why do they give permission for the officer to search it?" I'd been thinking about that question for a long time. I figured that the suspect assumed the officer would search the car anyway so he or she might as well cooperate.

"There are several likely reasons," Officer Collins begins, "People think that it's hidden so well that we won't find it, they don't want to appear guilty by denying us permission, and they think that if they give consent then we won't search it as thoroughly. Usually they plan on pleading ignorance to the drugs being hidden in the car if they're discovered, and other times they're just so nervous that they go along with the official request.   But even if we don't get permission from the driver, we have probable cause—that's a reasonable belief that a crime has been committed—so we'll most likely get a search warrant anyway. It'll just take longer."

Glancing over at me, Officer Collins continues. "Now, I was beginning to tell you about how police dogs are selected." (I sit on my hands.) "Sometimes people tell me that they think they might have a dog that would be a good candidate for drug detection or tracking. The first test is to find out how much they like to chase a ball or a toy. If the dog chases a ball until its tongue is about ready to fall off then an object like a metal pipe is substituted for the toy. Since dogs don't like to put metal in their mouth it's a real test to see if they're willing to pick it up and bring it back. The canine is also tested to see if it will retrieve an object from a place it's not comfortable going like water or thick bushes. If these tests are successful then the dog has displayed a level of obsession or skill that shows it may be suitable for police work.

"The most common breeds of dogs that are trained to find drugs are Belgian Malinois, Dutch shepherds and German shepherds. But it can be any breed of dog, from a Labrador to a Chihuahua." At the mention of a Chihuahua the students laugh collectively as they imagine the tiny animal in police action. The response from the students assures me that they indeed are listening. For a second I visualize a big, husky, uniformed officer at one end of the leash being tugged on by a single-minded Chihuahua barking, *"The marijuana's over here!"*

"Once a canine is identified who wants to play with an object all the time then the trainer begins using a little canvas bag as the dog's toy." At this point Officer Collins reaches behind his neck and, as if he were a magician, pulls out of the air a flesh-tone bag measuring about ten-by-four inches and a couple of inches thick.

"Inside the canvas bag is a plastic bag with the scent of marijuana in it," the sheriff's deputy explains. "This causes the dog being trained to learn to associate the scent with the toy. The trainer will throw the canvas bag while playing with the canine and soon the four-legged recruit learns that when he discovers the scent it means the toy is nearby. Since the toy is the most important thing in the world to my dog, he will search for it relentlessly in order to be able to play.

"Dogs can alert the handler to the scent of drugs by either passively sitting down or, in an aggressive manner barking, biting or scratching. In the case of Adam, we hide marijuana, and when he starts discovering where the marijuana smell is coming from he barks and we do nothing. He bites at the location and we do nothing. But when he first scratches at the spot then we immediately throw his toy down at his feet to reinforce his behavior. This is the procedure used repeatedly to train him to learn that if he wants to play with his toy he needs to discover the exact location of the scent.

"The drug dogs don't know that what they're doing has anything to do with drugs. But once they're trained to find their toy with the scent of marijuana then we can gradually introduce the dog to the smell of other drugs or narcotics that have different scents, like cocaine, heroin and meth.

"Adam is also trained to track people by their individual scent, but he's not trained in apprehension or handler protection work.

"Sarge, didn't the department have a K-9 years ago that was trained to apprehend fleeing subjects?"

"That's right," I confirm. "Twenty years ago there was a German shepherd named Yackel Von Baerenzwinger. For good reason he was called by his first name, Yackel. Besides being trained to locate drugs he protected his handler, could chase down suspects and locate them when they were hiding. I remember one night on third shift our detail responded to a silent alarm at the Brown Wheel Tavern where we knew at least one burglar was holed up. The after-hours visitor had started to leave through the rear door but quickly changed his mind and direction after facing two barrels from a deputy's shotgun.

"Yackel and his handler found the suspect hiding in the attic under some insulation. Later that night, after the arrest, I walked up to the K-9 officer's patrol car to congratulate him. Then I did something stupid. Although the entire department had been cautioned not to make any aggressive movements towards the handler, in my excitement, I forgot.

"I told the officer, sitting in his car, 'good job' as I slapped him firmly on the shoulder. Yackel rose up, gave a deep, fierce growl and prepared to jump through the front seat window from his position in the rear seat. The handler immediately ordered him to stop as I quickly withdrew my hand and gave a nervous laugh."

After my story the students start raising their hands with questions. Officer Collins welcomes this transition before getting Adam from his patrol unit.

"Does Adam live at the police station?" asks one curious member of the audience.

"No, he lives with me and my family. He gets time off from work just like the other officers."

Another hand goes up as the student blurts out, "Does Adam have a bullet proof vest? I saw on TV where this K-9 had a bullet proof vest to protect him when he went into a house to search for criminals."

"Some K-9s do wear body armor to help protect them from getting injured or killed if they get shot, but Adam doesn't have a vest like that. We only use him to search for drugs when the situation is under our control. We don't send him into a building on his own to find someone that might be armed. I'm always with him when he's searching for drugs or people. This keeps him safer and it also allows me to testify in court to what he discovers on the premises."

"But what if Adam gets shot and killed?" the same student continues, completing his original thought.

"Then we'd have a police funeral for him and if we caught the person who shot him there would be criminal charges and penalties for harming our K-9. It's unlawful to inflict harm, permanent disability or death upon a police dog," Collins quotes from a state statute.

"What happens when Adam gets old or can't detect drugs anymore?" inquires another student who could someday be a retirement planner.

I wonder the same thing. After years of service surely the dog wouldn't be abandoned, but on the other hand I can't imagine a Kansas Police and Fire canine retirement plan supported by the County Commissioners.

Deputy Collins explains, "On other departments that have had dogs retire from active duty the handler is often given the first opportunity to adopt his partner into his home as a family member. Actually K-9s make great pets and are usually good with children. You can imagine how willing they are to play while retrieving a ball or other toy."

As Collins describes the advantage to children I wonder how the canine would adapt to a household without a lot of activity. Wouldn't he go stir crazy?

"How much did he cost?" is another pertinent question that interests me.

"His purchase price, including his training to detect drugs and track people was $10,000," responds Officer Collins.

"Whoa! Wow! 10,000 dollars!" the class of students react in disbelief. I feel myself choking.

Deputy Collins is unapologetic about the price. "There's a community group of business people concerned about the dangers of illegal drugs harming our children. They want to help make a difference. They donated the money to purchase Adam for the Sheriff's Department. There's also a local veterinarian that donates his services for Adam's health care. We are clearly fortunate to have citizens that do more than talk about the drug problem."

"How long does a K-9 work looking for drugs before he gets tired?" questions another student.

"Dogs are kind of like people in that it all depends on the working conditions and their drive or eagerness to get the job done. And dogs, like people, need breaks from constantly being on alert. They also need success to find their toy once in awhile. Otherwise they feel like giving up. When Adam is searching a large building I can tell when he's starting to get tired. I let him find his toy so he can have a break."

Then the school's assistant principal, who has a photo of her black Labrador on her office desk, jumps into our discussion. "When we have our school searched for drugs, sometimes Officer Collins and Adam will have another K-9 team work with them. That way they can quickly check all the lockers while classes are in session. Having two drug dogs working at the same time helps prevent fatigue," she accurately states, reinforcing Officer Collins' previous answer.

Unable to keep my mouth shut and inappropriately trying to be funny about a serious subject, I add, "I sure hope none of you students has drugs on you today!"

The administrator puts me in my place. "What do you mean 'today'? None of you should be using drugs any day. It's not smart or healthy to use drugs and you can get caught. The high school also has regular searches for drugs by the K-9s. They even check the cars in the parking lot."

I like the way she is informative and at the same time proactive about the use of drugs. She lets them know while they are in middle school that the entire district is doing its best to keep the educational establishment a drug-free zone.

Finally, a student asks the question everyone else has been eager for: "When will we get to see Adam?"

Officer Collins glances at the clock and answers, "I'll go get him as soon as I explain what's going to happen when we return. First off, is there anyone here scared of dogs they don't know?"

"No," is the unanimous answer.

"Second, when we come in the room Adam will be anxious to find his toy. Sergeant Potter, with the school administration's permission, has hidden some drugs in the room for Adam to try to locate. When he detects the drugs he will paw at the location and I will reward him with his toy.

"Last thing is, please don't pet him if he walks past you. I'll let you pet him towards the end of the class if you want. Does everyone understand?" he concludes.

The class says they understand, then visibly grow eager to finally meet Officer Collins' partner. As the K-9 officer heads out the door to the parking lot I stand up and say, "Now I can tell you a story about Officer Collins."

I explain to the class that not only do the K-9s need to be trained, but the handlers too have to be certified in their knowledge and performance. Then I tell a story about Officer Collins' first day on the job with Adam when they were invited to participate in an actual search warrant. It was a house where the officers were looking for illegal drugs.

"When the newly trained team of two first entered the suspect's house through the kitchen door Adam headed directly for the trash can. There, clearly visible, was a partially eaten hamburger resting on top of a McDonald's® sack.

"Officer Collins was disappointed in Adam, especially after all their training, that he would be so unfocused on drugs but excited by food. So, as Adam kept pulling towards the trash can Collins pulled him back, called him off and took him into another room to begin a calmer search. Adam eventually did discover drugs in an upstairs bedroom drawer, but the biggest stash was found by a detective searching the trash. Inside the McDonald's® sack, which was under the partially eaten hamburger in the kitchen, was a sizeable amount of methamphetamine. Officer Collins learned that very first day to trust Adam's drug detecting abilities even when it might appear that the canine was off track."

Just then Adam appears at the classroom doorway with his handler a leash behind. Adam is straining to get into action, to find his toy, as the students give a collective sigh of, "Isn't he cute!" Officer Collins begins walking backwards, encouraging Adam to search high and low as they traverse around the perimeter of the classroom. They work a bookcase, teacher's desk and a metal filing cabinet before Adam stops, then starts pawing at a cabinet door as if to say, *"I found my toy!"* Immediately Officer Collins reaches up behind his neck and throws Adam's canvas bag at the dog's feet. Adam quickly chomps on it, his head tossing side to side displaying great excitement at his discovery.

As Adam plays, Officer Collins recovers the green leafy substance in a plastic bag and secures it in a tightly fitting plastic container. Then he plays a bit with Adam, grabbing each end of the canvas bag while it is strongly gripped in Adam's mouth, lifting the K-9 a foot off the floor. At this the students again laugh, appreciating the dog's determination to hold on to its toy. But, when ordered, Adam gives up his most prized possession to his handler. They play toss and fetch together before it's time to give the students an opportunity to pet Adam. It seems everyone wants to touch him, including the assistant principal.

The police dog named Adam is clearly a welcome change to the sometimes sterile school environment. Adam and Officer Collins are ambassadors, a bridge connecting law enforcement with the youth of the school community. Working together they are making a difference.

11

CERTAINTY AND UNCERTAINTY[15]

"DO YOU LIKE YOUR JOB?"

"Sergeant Potter, do you like your job?"
"Oh, yes! Can't you tell?"
"I thought you did, but I was just wondering because I don't always like school."

"When I was your age I didn't always like school, especially when I didn't understand assignments or when I flunked a test. Sometimes it seemed impossible."

"Do you have fun at work?"

"Well, I enjoy what I'm doing, but I usually wouldn't call it fun. When I visit your class and we discuss your safety and making good decisions, that's important to me. I feel really good when I'm able to help in the learning process. I feel rewarded when I'm working with people, especially youth, helping contribute to your development. I find that my growth is reflected in your growth."

"What about recess? Is that fun for you?"

"Okay, now we're talking! Yes, it's fun! It's

a pleasure playing outside with your class. When I hit a home run playing kickball I'm one happy cop!"

"My mom reminds me all the time that when we're in middle school we don't get recess anymore."

"She's right. I guess school is getting you ready for being an adult. Most jobs don't include a recess unless you're a school teacher or like me, a school resource officer. The playground teachers don't usually play in a game because they're watching out for everyone's safety. And, with my busy schedule I can't really get out to recess very often, maybe that's why I enjoy it so much when I do get it!"

"Have you arrested anyone today?"

"No, not even close. It's been a long time. I mostly teach and go to meetings rather than write tickets or take people to jail."

"What about when you first became a deputy? Was that fun?"

"It was exciting and stressful but, again, I'm not sure about fun. One of the first jobs I had to learn was being an emergency dispatcher on the police radio and I wasn't very good at that. That was not fun! Good thing I got to go out on the road as a patrol officer. Working the road I was able to make things happen, like catching a speeder, discovering someone driving on a suspended license or finding a drunk driver. I wasn't constantly responding to emergency telephone calls or officer requests. Nor was I trapped in a windowless room for the entire shift."

"My father has a police scanner in his truck."

"You know, more and more officers and 911 dispatchers are communicating on their computers by sending text messages. But, when I started as a rookie officer I could barely understand the people talking to one another over the radio. It was a different language to me and I questioned my fitness for the job. I felt like I was a foreigner in a strange land with 'un poco' language skills. I didn't have experience listening to or talking on citizen band radios (CBs), but I purchased a scanner so that I could practice hearing the broadcast conversations. I'm sure the other officers got pretty tired of me asking them to repeat what they said. Gradually, I gained experience and confidence, but for awhile I thought it was going to kill me first. It sure taught me to appreciate dispatchers."

"Sometimes school is boring. You must never be bored when you're arresting people and getting into car chases?"

"I think the reason I don't get bored is because I have an active imagination, a strong work ethic and I understand the possibilities of my job. Working as a patrol officer offered me a lot of variety in my assignments and investigations. Each traffic stop gave me the opportunity (probable cause) to see what else I could learn from a public encounter. Did the driver have a valid driver's license or was it suspended or revoked? Was there a warrant out for the driver or for a passenger? Was the vehicle insured? Was the driver drunk or drugged? Could we spot an open container, drugs or drug paraphernalia in the vehicle? Occasionally, we even stopped a stolen automobile or got into a car chase, causing our adrenalin to flow. Each vehicle stop was an opportunity for us to develop our observation and personal safety skills. We were always learning."

"I've been in our car before when my dad got stopped for speeding."

"How did that go? What happened?"

"My dad said he'd pay the ticket, but he thought it was too much money."

"They are expensive."

"Do you get to keep the money?"

"Oh, no! Your dad didn't give the money to the officer, he probably paid it through the mail or stopped in at the court house. Most of the money goes to the county and some of it to the state. I guess part of it, in a way, may help pay our wages."

"My dad still speeds sometimes when we're late for ball practice or church."

"Yeah, most people seem like they're always in a hurry. When I write someone a speeding ticket I'm trying to help teach them a lesson. I want to try and prevent a traffic accident caused by unsafe driving. I feel it's my chance to help the community. Speed does kill. My hope is that at some point a driver might figure out that slowing down is cheaper than paying tickets, and that it can prevent his or her driver's license from being suspended or taken away."

"Do you like writing speeding tickets?"

"When I was out on patrol I liked catching people. My belief was that anyone that got caught deserved it and had a chance to learn from it. I was always trying to catch drunk drivers before they got into a wreck and injured or killed someone. Catching people satisfied me. There was certainty and uncertainty in every traffic stop. I also received significance from my peers and connection with them because of my arrests. I felt accomplished the more I experienced (and survived) different encounters while refining my techniques for enforcing the law."

"Do you have to catch people to keep your job? What if you don't see anyone breaking the law?"

"We don't have a quota system that requires us to write a set number of tickets or make a certain number of arrests in order to keep our job. But, if an officer never wrote a ticket or made an arrest then the other officers, including the supervisors, would give the deputy a hard time for being lazy or for not having any initiative. There are people breaking the law a lot so it would be pretty hard, day after day, to not catch anyone. But officers also work traffic accidents, check buildings and take reports of crimes being committed. We do more than arrest people."

"Why did you stop being a patrol officer?"

"After seven years of working patrol (four of which I was a supervisor) I began to notice that patrolling the road was less rewarding to me. Writing people tickets wasn't as important as it had been. I started giving drivers more breaks on infractions than I had in the past. It was a sign of job burnout. I needed a change. Maybe I was tiring of the offenders who didn't learn from their encounters with the law. Some called it revolving door justice and, if you can imagine it, they'd even forget to thank me for writing them a speeding ticket or taking them to jail!

"Maybe it was too little sleep during the day as I tried to attend family activities and a part-time job before working patrol all night. It was a paradox that my conscientiousness to attend these social events had a negative result as it affected my alertness, patience and good humor both on and off the job. I was trying to do too much. Maybe it was the stress of one too many crime scenes. Especially the ones where I was emotionally involved with the victims and their survivors after fatality car wrecks and scenes of suicide."

"How did you become a school resource officer?"

"The administration at our department decided to create a full-time position to work in the schools, I was selected for my enthusiasm and experience. I had not sought the job, but it was perfect for the department, the community and for me! I quickly recognized that my personal and professional needs could again be met in this new job assignment! I was back in familiar territory—teaching, only now I was in uniform. Was this something teachers dreamed about in unruly classrooms, wearing a loaded gun with the power to arrest disorderly students?"

* * *

Today, as a school resource officer I have plenty of certainty and uncertainty during my shift to keep me interested and challenged. I sleep at night and work during the day! Phone calls rarely interrupt my active dream state. I never think twice about what I'm going to wear each morning or which vehicle I'm going to drive to work. I can take a day off if it fits into my schedule. I visit many schools, sometimes on a weekly basis for set classes like Drug Abuse Resistance Education©, Social Problems and Solutions, or Life Skills. During these educational encounters I'm a familiar face, welcomed by students, teachers and staff. But besides the scheduled school visits, bringing prisoners to court or monthly community board meetings, I have plenty of other responsibilities.

A principal may want my assistance or advice on a school crime while a student may ask me to shoot baskets at recess. I may be speaking about school crisis plans one day and methamphetamine awareness the next. I might be working with my fellow SROs, planning a fund-raiser or searching for camp counselors to help with that annual event. My day is full of both my planned schedule and surprises.

In the back of my mind I recognize that there's always the possibility that my day will be interrupted by gunfire—mine or someone else's. Gunfire is an unknown that, because of its rarity can create shock and turmoil in any officer's life. But most of my diversity on the job comes from preparing a multitude of lessons for different demographics, never knowing how well the audience will receive my message, always striving to listen, learn and improve.

Actually, just as there are never routine traffic stops, there is never a routine school visit. I may teach a class I've taught fifty times over fifteen years, but for me each class, each interaction, is different and carries with it a life-changing opportunity for me and the students. This is true because not only have I learned something new between visits but the youth are usually fresh to this classroom experience. Being a resource from outside the school, I enter the educational establishment with a perspective based on my many law enforcement adventures. I'm an authority figure, but I'm not an authority on everything. The students teach me all the time.

Many centered individuals explain that we are not what we do, but every day that I wear my uniform, complete with badge and gun and drive to work in a marked patrol car, reminds me of the importance of my work. I feel significant. After years of working in the same schools, building relationships, watching the children grow up and helping them turn abstract ideas into concrete thinking, I feel like a real part of the community. When I assist the public, young and old, I feel that I've made a contribution. It keeps me alive. I'm fulfilled in my work.

"Do you like your job?"

"Yes, it's the best job on the department for me because I get to work with young people in areas of youth development, education and prevention. I'm eternally grateful for the opportunity to serve my community."

12

CAREER PATH

"WHAT DO I HAVE TO DO TO BECOME A POLICE OFFICER?"

*"So, how many officers on your department?"
the Reno County Sheriff asks the Captain from
the LAPD (Los Angeles Police Department) while
attending the F.B.I. National Academy.*

*"Approximately ninety-one hundred," answers
the Captain. "How about your department?" he
continues.*

"Eighty-one," states the Sheriff.

*"Oh, eighty-one hundred is a pretty good
size."*

"No, we have a total of 81."

[Silence. Then laughter from the Captain.]

*A New York City officer then jumps into the
conversation: "We have over 35,000 officers."* [16]

————

In my e-mail there was a request for my time:
"Can you help us with a career day at the
high school?" I checked my calendar. "Yes,"
was my one-word response. When the event
was closer we'd discuss particulars.

Whether they're children, teens or young
adults, sooner or later I hear the question:

"What would I have to do to become a police officer?" Once I hear the inquiry I usually take a deep breath, wondering where to begin. In processing the question I speculate on how detailed an answer they want. I mean, we could be here awhile.

If there's plenty of time I might ask the inquirer how they got interested in police work or what intrigues them about the profession. Then we can have a discussion. Often I'll learn that they have a relative or a friend who has told them exciting stories, creating curiosity about the work. But more often I'll be told that a popular TV cop show has enticed them to consider the life of a crime scene investigator.

If I only have a couple of seconds to answer the question I'll say, "stay out of trouble and get a good education." Those few words speak volumes. Once a young person begins to get into trouble they may keep going down that familiar marked path. They may also be labeled by others as a "trouble-maker," making it all the more difficult to alter their course into police work.

I explain to my students straightforwardly that once a person has a felony conviction as an adult, then they've thrown away the opportunity to be a law enforcement officer. One bad choice can prevent an individual from obtaining a job that they might have excelled at, tremendously enjoyed, and in which the community might have greatly benefited.

We also talk about how, when juveniles start breaking the law, they don't automatically stop when they turn eighteen, because by then it's become a way of life. By then they've usually surrounded themselves with a cast of like-minded characters with similar, questionable values and behaviors.

I'm big on education and developing a love of learning. If the student asking me how to become a police officer thinks that this career choice will allow her to avoid academic work, they're quickly disappointed with my response. I like to explain that being a deputy sheriff is more complex than drinking coffee and eating donuts during a car chase. I emphasize just how much paperwork is required when we investigate a crime or make an arrest.

Every case has the potential, however unlikely, of going all the way to the United States Supreme Court. What's more likely to happen is that an officer will need to testify to what he observed at a crime scene and what was said in an interview, even if the event took place months or even years before the criminal or civil trial. There have been many times, when without rereading my detailed offense report, I wouldn't have had a clue how to answer a specific question raised by a prepared defense attorney. Thank goodness I learned to take good notes.

There's so much advice I can give to students interested in law enforcement. It's all based on my opinion, experience and values. After years of being a Boy Scout my bias is that every potential recruit should be "trustworthy, loyal, helpful, friendly, courteous, kind, obedient, cheerful, thrifty, brave, clean and reverent."[17] As an adult I still think they're great traits to have, with the possible exception of obedient. By this I mean that there are circumstances where blindly following a command could be unwise, unethical or illegal. Yet, in reality, there comes a time, especially in an emergency when there's no time for discussion. Clearly, making appropriate decisions is the most important part of working in law enforcement.

One thing that I often hear in law enforcement is that "common sense can't be taught," yet it is a requirement for the job. Unfortunately, what one person considers common sense another person may interpret as bizarre behavior. If a driver won't pull over for an officer in his marked patrol car, emergency lights flashing and siren wailing, yes, there is cause for concern. But if the speeding vehicle being pursued is maintaining a steady speed, has its hazard lights blinking, is not trying to evade the officer, and is approaching the local hospital, then one needs to start figuring that there *may* be a legitimate reason the driver won't pull over. When the car finally does turn into the hospital's property, stops near the emergency room entrance, and the driver exits the vehicle, he shouldn't be surprised if the officer is cautious, even aggressive, before being helpful.

Our ultimate challenge as officers is to use common sense but at the same time to be equally prepared for the worse scenario. Citizens want us to be safe, but they don't always realize what that entails. Sometimes what we do to increase our security is inconvenient or upsetting to them. Could the pursued driver have recently committed armed robberies, be afraid of arrest and desperate enough to shoot the officer? Yes, but the public expects us to be professional, empathetic to their emergencies and to have, you guessed it, common sense. We should know that they're at the emergency room for an emergency!

But we law enforcement officers already know from experience that some of the people we deal with don't have common sense (by our definition) and that they blatantly, repeatedly, lie to our face! Some, falling down drunk, will swear to God, and at us, that they only had two beers to drink. Others will deny they burglarized a business despite the facts: 1) we have their full-color video mug-shot taken during the crime by multiple security cameras, 2) at the police interview the suspect is still wearing the identical clothing he wore in the captured image, and 3) his misplaced wallet with identification was discovered at the crime scene!

The longer we do our job the better prepared we should be to expect anything, including the unusual, from the general public. But that expectation comes at a risk: that we become jaded, judgmental, suspicious that everyone is a cheat, liar or a criminal. Sometimes it's a difficult balance between reacting and overreacting in our business, even with common sense.

Not everyone can or should be an officer. I have high professional expectations from everyone who wears the badge. I want police officers who are fair, smart, flexible, know what they're doing, have exceptional values (especially integrity), are in good physical condition and are approachable. Their mission, I hope, includes a passion for justice, to help everyone, including those who look and act differently than they. Since officers have the power to arrest and to use lethal force I also expect them to unfailingly maintain a standard of obeying the laws they enforce—being drug and trouble-free. Officers need to walk their talk.

When I say someone should be approachable I mean that their personality should welcome others to dialogue, to not be arrogant or condescending. There is no room for prejudice and discrimination when dealing with the very people we are entrusted to serve. We work for people of every race, religion and nationality, from all income levels, who speak any language, of both genders, with whatever sexuality they claim or learning ability they possess.

Being open to others is vital to effective communication skills. Someone considering law enforcement must be able to listen well and explain carefully, patiently and comfortably. An officer must be assertive and authoritative but also have the ability to be caring. He should understand the need to have a tender and compassionate approach when the situation calls for it, especially with children.

Outstanding officers must work both independently and interdependently. As much as I enjoy working autonomously I know that without teamwork, big, important jobs won't get done. Officers are also required to accomplish a great deal of work on their own, from initiating traffic stops to deciding when to give a citizen the benefit of a doubt. When you have a large county with only a few officers available during a shift, you need to quickly learn to take care of yourself. That is your number one priority. But when you develop an ability to sense when one of your team members is in potential trouble then you become invaluable.

Good officers are problem-solvers. They don't just document problems. They must be creative and ingenious in finding solutions. One avenue is bringing education to the community in the form of Neighborhood Watch, action committees or by facilitating mediation. The best resolution could be contacting outside agencies that can study a reoccurring problem. For example, if on an officer's beat there is an intersection where there are reoccurring wrecks, an observant deputy will contact the public works department to assess the traffic problem. An engineer might improve the intersection design with a properly placed traffic signal. Hopefully, government officials can facilitate a solution beyond simply budgeting for more ambulances and hiring additional EMT's to work accidents. A little effort on the part of an officer can make a big difference.

I don't dwell on it when I'm speaking to the public, but anyone going into law enforcement needs to be prepared for the fact that they will work scenes involving the dead and the dying. Most likely the deceased person will be a stranger, but there is the possibility that she could be a friend or relative. Death is always lurking. It comes with the job. It's one of the stressors, along with unusual working hours and unusual people. An officer must accept and deal with death or it can create problems on and off the job. I'm still unclear about how to better prepare recruits for the times when they will encounter stiff or decomposed and putrid bodies. For me, having spiritual faith goes a long way toward accepting death, but that didn't prevent grisly death scenes from being a stressor in my life during my patrol duty days.

Sometimes students tell me that they want to be a detective. I explain to them that they won't pick up a newspaper and find the job opening listed in the classified ads. At our department, newly hired employees begin their work in the jail where they meet many a criminal they may later arrest on new charges. A successful candidate for detective must have the inclination, personality and the patience to wait for openings to develop. Detectives are universally promoted from within their agency after years of working the streets in the patrol division.

One size department does not fit all. Applicants must consider which size suits their career plans. In a larger department, even though promotions may be more competitive, there's a chance for varied specialization such as traffic scene investigator, K-9 officer, school resource officer, emergency response team member, hostage negotiator and rangemaster. Some officers will prefer the dynamics of a smaller department with a slower pace, less hierarchy and a more personal relationship to the community.

When I attended the F.B.I. National Academy in Quantico, Virginia, I was told that all the newly hired agents graduated college, but most of them did not major in criminal justice. That surprised me. Instead, many of them specialized in law, accounting or finance, physical science, engineering and foreign languages. Those skills are more helpful in investigating white collar crime and in collecting intelligence.

Speaking with high school students at career days I'm quick to tell the group that I have one wish for them. "I wish that you'll all find a job that is the right fit for you, one that you can enjoy, that will be fulfilling for you. There are too many people who hate their job and I feel sorry for each one of them. Life's too short to spend so much of your day or night working at a job that you dislike." We also talk about money. "You'll never get rich on a deputy's pay," I say as I hand out a flyer from our agency explaining starting salary, benefits and minimum requirements.

I've had eager individuals tell me that first they plan on earning a college degree in criminal justice, then attending the law enforcement academy in order to be hired as a police officer. I break the bad news. In Kansas and in most other states, you have to be hired first before you can attend the academy. The minimum requirements for our department include:

- U.S. citizenship.
- Be at least nineteen years of age to work the jail (minimum age of twenty-one to attend the law enforcement academy in order to work patrol).
- High school graduate or General Equivalency Diploma (G.E.D.).
- Valid Kansas driver's license.
- No felony or domestic violence convictions.

Most state and federal law enforcement agencies (highway patrol, F.B.I., A.T.F.) require a four-year college degree for new hires, but local departments have a wider range of minimum educational standards. The dilemma faced by the city and county governments that are less populated is that they lack a sufficient budget to offer a wage that will attract the candidate. However, applicants with a diploma will always have a distinct advantage in the hiring process and throughout their career as they compete within the department for promotions.

Besides the entrance exam, which tests one's knowledge of grammar, math, reading and comprehension, eligible applicants are required to successfully pass a background check, oral interview, drug screen and psychological exam. Most departments also have a physical agility test and at least a one mile timed run as part of their entry requirements. So, the overall message I convey at career fairs is that "by paying attention, studying in school and keeping in good physical shape you're already preparing to pass the entrance test to begin your career in law enforcement. You don't need to wait until you're older. You can start right now."

There are many young, impressive candidates begging for a job in law enforcement, but they don't get hired because another candidate has more experience. On our department we've hired young men and women who have previously participated in our law enforcement cadet post. Those youth, ages sixteen through twenty, get a diverse look at the world of law enforcement. They attend regular training meetings, participate in the ride-along program where they are teamed up with officers on duty and help at special events. The cadets wear police uniforms with a duty belt that holds a walkie-talkie, flashlight, handcuffs but no firearm and have security clearance throughout the building. Being a cadet is a valuable opportunity for any young person wishing to learn if he or she is suitable for a career in law enforcement, while providing a valuable service to the community. It's also a chance for a mentor to materialize in their new vocation.

Another advantage of becoming a cadet is the opportunity to learn if the work is fulfilling to them. Do you know anyone who has repeatedly changed their major in college? It can be an expensive and stressful process of searching for a direction that feels right. That's why it's crucial to know as soon as possible what you *don't* want to do, so you can discover what you *do* want to do.

Prior to my junior year in college I had to decide between forestry and teaching. In order to discover if forestry was my passion I worked for the summer on a work crew at the Red River Ranger Station in Idaho. It was beautiful scenery, but it wasn't the job I expected. Upon eliminating this outdoor profession from my dream list, I returned to Illinois and majored in history so I could teach. Never during my college career at Southern Illinois University did I dream I'd ever be a deputy sheriff!

Before discovering my career path I worked as a store security officer, counselor's aide at a Georgia prison, school teacher and coach in the public schools in Illinois, as a school teacher at our local (State of Kansas) prison and as a substance abuse counselor. The value of my different jobs is that not only did I gain life experiences and test my interests, but I also established an excellent employment record. Each stop was another credential that documented my work skills and connected me with an individual I could later rely on to be a reference to my character and professionalism. All of my work preceding my employment as a deputy sheriff prepared me for the competitive application and interview process. I had not been wasting my time.

One area that I thought I was deficient in, that I thought might hurt my chances of being hired, was firearms. My only experience with shooting a weapon was a .22 rifle at Scout camp! Surely, I worried, I'd be a joke next to ex-military officers who had already been in life and death fire fights. But I was relieved to hear in the interview process that firearm training was done on the job, and that the rangemaster preferred working with people who had not already developed bad habits. That was me!

When I speak about my law enforcement profession I share the fact that four times a year we are tested at the firearm's range to make sure we are still proficient. Officers are required to maintain their accuracy or risk losing their job.

I remember my own applicant interview that took place twenty-five years ago. I didn't have any knowledge of the questions I'd be asked, but I practiced answering one anticipated question: "If necessary, will you be able to use deadly force?" In other words, "Was I prepared to kill someone?" Having never even pointed a real gun at anyone, I sure couldn't speak from experience so I answered the question the best I could. "Yes, of course, if it was justified," I said, hoping I sounded more confident than I was feeling.

It seemed more important to me to be sure that I didn't kill someone that *didn't* deserve to die. Later, at the academy we learned a great deal about the force continuum, how only as much force as is necessary should be used to control a situation. We were trained in "shoot, don't shoot" scenarios using a video projected on the classroom wall. It taught us up close and personal that we had better be sure of ourselves in any possible lethal encounter, because once you fire a bullet you can never take it back. Throughout my career I've thought about how paralyzing a "bad shoot" would be to me. I'd hate to be haunted the rest of my life with that unforgettable memory of killing or maiming an innocent person.

One of the last things I do when I'm speaking to high school students at career fairs is to encourage them to find out as much as they can about the work. Investigate. Talk to officers. Visit a police station. Ride with different officers if administrative approval can be obtained. Observe. Ask more questions. Become a cadet if an explorer post is in their geographical area. Don't depend on TV as your only source of information. Show initiative.

I assure the students that if they decide to test the waters of law enforcement, they will receive a great deal of training both within their agency and at the academy. They don't need to be experts beforehand. We know it can be overwhelming, but we don't want them to be overwhelmed. It's our job to protect new recruits from getting into situations that are over their heads. We want them to learn to swim, but we don't want them to drown. We know they are beginners. We want the job to be a perfect fit. We want them to be successful. When that happens...we all benefit.

13

A PERFECT PATROL DEPUTY DAY[18]

"HAVE YOU EVER DREAMED ABOUT YOUR JOB AS A POLICE OFFICER?"

"Sergeant Potter, have you ever dreamed about your job as a police officer?" I'm asked by a student in class who is researching a famous person for a biography report.

"Yes, sometimes I do dream about my job. My dreams are usually about being on patrol or teaching in the classrooms as a school resource officer."

"Will you tell us about a dream you've had?"

"Sure. This one is a recurring dream I have about a day at work. Let me tell you about it."

———

O600 – I awake to the aroma of home made cinnamon rolls and baked apples. I hear my wife, Alex, in the kitchen singing: "Oh, what a beautiful morning, oh, what a beautiful day."

0605 – Alex enters with my breakfast along with the morning paper, *The Hutchinson News.* I enjoy my meal propped up in bed while Alex runs my bath water to the perfect temperature. The paper has great coverage on the success of the special mill levy passed to build the Justice Center. I think about how someday I'll be moving out of my closet office, avoiding filing cabinets in the hallways to work in a room that doesn't flood when it rains, ruining records and destroying supplies. Someday I'll work in an environment where employees and citizens can approach a bathroom door without an out of order sign posted or without the putrid smells from backed up toilets in an unsafe, poorly ventilated jail.

I notice an article in the newspaper about a local automobile dealership who is donating a new Corvette to the department to be used as an undercover vehicle. Free insurance, vehicle maintenance and unlimited gasoline are included in the dealership's contribution. On a national issue, the newspaper reports about the Supreme Court making it illegal for criminals to have more rights than their victims.

0620 – The bath water is ready. During my bath the radio announcer reads some of the articles I've just finished, then describes the apprehension of two career criminals by third-shift sheriff's deputies. The crooks had been discovered the night before inside a local school where they weren't taking evening classes. The reporter at the scene informs his radio audience that the burglars have admitted to the crime. They are quoted as stating, "We're guilty. We deserve to be caught for this and all the other undetected crimes we've committed in the past. This serves us right and we're sorry."

0630 – After my bath, I dry and dress. My ten-year-old son, Daniel, has voluntarily polished my boots. I find that my daughter, Sarah, has made sure that my shirt's badge, name tag and chevrons are properly attached.

0635 – I walk outside to my brand new special police package patrol car that has been assigned to me. Though it's not fully light outside, I shade my eyes from the sparkling surface. *"Who's been waxing it for me?"* I wonder. The car starts immediately at the turn of the key and the engine roars to life, purrs then hums.

0637 – A few miles from home, just inside the city limits, I observe an abandoned vehicle on the side of the road, so I request dispatch to check the registration. I'm informed that the automobile is a "hit" on N.C.I.C. (National Crime Information Center). Dispatch advises me that the local city officers will be in route immediately to thoroughly process the stolen vehicle.

0639 – After the PD's arrival, I continue towards the law enforcement center (LEC) for the morning detail meeting.

0640 – As I drive through Hutchinson in route to the briefing, I observe that the traffic is moving in an intelligent and courteous manner. I'm making all the green lights, too!

0641 – I pull the patrol unit into the parking place immediately in front of the entrance to the cleaners. An employee runs out, greets me and hands me my clean uniform that I dropped off the night before.

0642 – I pull away from the cleaners and make two more green traffic lights. Just after I pass the railroad tracks I notice in my rear view mirror that the light signals begin to flash and the gates start lowering.

0643 – Another green light and I pull into the LEC parking lot. I advise dispatch I'm "10-19" and immediately hear a cheerful, "10-4, 422, KNEL292." The basement door opens and I park the patrol unit in the stall nearest the patrol rooms. A painted sign on the wall informs all: "PARKING FOR SGT. JIM POTTER —ALL OTHER VEHICLES TOWED AT DRIVER'S EXPENSE." Bill and Darrel greet me as I hand over my car keys. Bill pops the hood to give the vehicle its morning maintenance check. Darrel turns the water hose on to begin washing the vehicle after noticing that some dust has settled on the rear bumper.

On the way to the detail room a patrol officer stops me and thanks me for the written reprimand he received the day before.

"Sarge," he says, "it's just what I needed to help me open my eyes and realize this job means a lot to me. I'm eager to make the necessary changes, to give the extra effort, so that I can continue to grow as a professional and be a better person."

I'm pleased to hear that the reprimand has been accepted with such a positive attitude so I congratulate the officer for his open mindedness.

0645 – I sit down at the patrol sergeant desk and sip a cold glass of orange juice that has been brought to me by the third shift, on-duty detective. After exchanging cordial greetings of "Great morning!" among first shift officers the detail meeting begins.

I read the case patrol log for entries reported since yesterday afternoon and see nothing particularly unusual: trash dumping on Pennington Rd., traffic complaint in Pretty Prairie, dog complaint at Westside Villa, neighborhood disturbance in Partridge, disturbance (love triangle) on East 4th, criminal damage to property (mailboxes) on 56th street, recovered stolen vehicle from the bottom of Cheney Reservoir, and five arrests—two for burglary at a rural school and three for DUI, one of which was the result of a non-injury car wreck where the drunken driver ran into a horse and buggy near Yoder.

I then read the assignments that were "no cased": cattle on roadway at 56th & Wilson Rd., llamas on roadway on Nickerson Blvd., grass fire on the railroad tracks at K-61 and US-50, west junction, and finally, alarm #2.

Beat assignments are given. Two traffic officers will work school zones and motor vehicle accidents. Four regulars and four reserves are paired up for their duties, one car per beat.

There is little time remaining before hitting the street, but I begin to read out loud a recent court decision from a monthly law and order publication entitled *Cuff and Stuff*. The case summary advises that a police department in Goodness, Arizona has been awarded $500,000 as reimbursement for court costs and officer suffering. It successfully overturned a civil suit filed against the department for false arrest. The summary concludes: "Due to the unreasonable mental anguish and pressure put upon Officer Wright, the court orders that the aforementioned police department provide said officer and family an all expense paid two-week vacation, for the purposes of special rest and recuperation, in order to enable said officer an opportunity to reflect and recharge before returning to duty."

The officers present at our detail meeting begin to applaud and cheer. They are hurrying out the door and down the hallway, still excited, racing to get to their patrol units and their respective beats. Each one wants to be an agent of social change for the betterment of the community they serve and protect. As the cheering fades, it turns to a...Zzzzzzzzzzzzz... Rrring! (Alarm goes off!)

0445 – I've been dreaming. Time to get up and get ready for work!

"But then," I tell the high school student, "after I've turned off the alarm and I've gotten up, I realize I'm still in the dream."

"Very interesting," remarks the young scholar.

"What do you think it means?" I ask.

"I'm not sure yet," the serious student replies, puzzled, "I still need to do more reading."

"Who are you studying?" I ask.

"Sigmund Freud, the father of psychology. He wrote a book titled *The Interpretation of Dreams*. He believed that our dreams are a blend of our wishes and our recent experiences."

"Hmmm," is all I can muster, wondering if I've told her too much. *"Wasn't Freud the father of* abnormal *psychology?"* I think to myself. I begin to worry.

"Is there anything wrong? What are you thinking?" she inquires.

"That I better go read Sigmund Freud before the department gives me a psychological test.

There's a saying in law enforcement that if you aren't crazy when you get hired into this profession that you'll be crazy by the time you get out of it."

14

LESSONS LEARNED

"CAN I TRY ON YOUR HANDCUFFS?"

Children (boys) at school: *"Will you handcuff me? Please!"*
Adult going to jail: *"Do you have to handcuff me? I'll cooperate. I promise."*

On this particular winter day a boy with exploring eyes, a perpetual grin, and an active imagination asked me if he could see my handcuffs. I thought about it for a second, realized we had a few minutes before the next bell and took the seldom used silver bracelets out of my simulated leather case which always resided on my duty belt.

"Here you go, Joseph," presenting the sought-after accoutrement. As I handed him the cuffs his eyes got even bigger. He didn't say anything, but he was already energetically thinking. He walked away, melted away, escaping to a corner of the room, inspecting the borrowed treasure in his own world. Seconds later, as my eyes refocused on his image, he was turned away from me. I saw his back and then observed his elbows. They told a story. I could see that his arms were parallel to the floor as he struggled to pull the manacles apart. Was he testing the strength of the steel links which connected the cloned bracelets? Or was he caught up in his fantasy world where Joseph's mighty mental focus, or some special super power was stronger than these standard police issue handcuffs?

In a minute reality returned as this kinesthetic learner was prepared to discover more answers to new questions. What was it like to wear real handcuffs? Could he escape from these even though the steel was not bending to his will? He approached me with the question I had anticipated, "Can I put them on?"

Normally my answer would have been easy. I had said it hundreds of times before. "I don't handcuff children." But I made an exception to my own rule because I understood that Joseph was a tactile learner and here was a chance for him to literally have a hands-on experience. *"What harm could it do?"* my mind quickly reasoned.

"Yes," I answered.

Another student, Jean, got in on the unofficial handcuffing, eager to participate in the evolving event, a rite representing power and control, fate and helplessness, or an occasion to contemplate changing one's direction in life. After I cautioned the two players about the risks of catching Joseph's skin in the moving metal, they appeared more focused and careful, with the female officer-in-training properly double-locking the cuffs with a nearby paperclip.

"Now, see if you can get out of them!" she challenged the excited Houdini, who explained that he used to buy plastic toy handcuffs and break out of them.

As soon as the cuffs had been clicked into a secure position I started my routine. "Oh, oh!" I began patting my pockets. "I'm sure I brought my handcuff key with me today, but where is it?" By this time a dozen classmates were in the room with half of them watching Joseph, the center of attention.

"What's going on here?"

"Oh, he's wearing Sergeant Potter's handcuffs!"

Pulling a single patrol car key from my pants pocket I continued my rehearsed search for my ring of keys, the ring that would lead to Joseph's return to a structured curriculum. "Oh, no! I can't find my handcuff key!" I announced, my voice gaining an octave of concern, unable to immediately locate the expected metal bulge anywhere in my pockets.

As I watched Joseph making fists, tensing his muscles, contorting his face, he continued attempting to break the links apart. He was savoring this moment, testing his theory. Here I had planned on significantly raising his stress level by pretending to have lost my handcuff key, and he couldn't have cared less! In fact, any delay on my part meant more time for him to invent further options for escape. Good thing he didn't have a fear of being confined. Ironically, I was the one that was now looking worried. Had I left my full set of keys at home during my lunch break before class? I wasn't pretending. I really couldn't find my keys!

As the bell rang, Mrs. Snyder entered the classroom, saw Joseph in handcuffs and looked directly at me. I said weakly, "We have a little problem. I can't find my handcuff key." She could have said, "What do you mean 'we'?" but she smiled, still waiting for me to tell her I was joking. As I double-checked my pockets, solemn, I informed her that my missing keys might be outside in my patrol unit or, at worse, at home.

We had all the students sit down at their desks, including Joseph. Mrs. Snyder prepared to start the lesson as I grabbed my coat for the trip outside. I wanted to reassure her and myself that things were still under control, but I was delaying the inevitable. I had to leave Joseph behind in our classroom in my handcuffs.

"I can always call dispatch and have them send an officer if I can't locate my keys...any standard handcuff key will work to open these up...it wouldn't be the first time someone has called 911 to have cuffs unlocked," I mumbled, in a lame attempt to recover my earlier confidence.

"Well, at least *I* didn't handcuff Joseph. He did it to himself," I whispered to Mrs. Snyder on my way out, totally minimizing that I was the officer, the so-called responsible adult, the teacher who turned over my handcuffs to a student during school hours and condoned, if not encouraged him to cuff himself.

But I needed to stop talking and solve the problem. I rushed from the school, efficiently searched my patrol unit, then sped away in route to my house only five miles down the road. I was in a hurry but still very careful about my driving—the last thing I needed was an accident. I was also attentive for any citizens that might see my patrol car challenging the speed limit. If I wasn't careful things could get worse.

As soon as I opened my front door at home I saw my keys staring at me from right where I had left them on the table. I took a second to locate the miniature key on the ring, but before hurrying out to the driveway said, "Thank you for small miracles." On my return trip to school, when I realized there was plenty of time before class was over, a thought struck me; *"I would play a prank on good natured Mrs. Snyder!"*

When I got back to the school office I asked Ruth, the secretary, if she would help me with a joke on my team teacher. I asked her to call Mrs. Snyder in her classroom and tell her to send Joseph to the office because his mother was there to take him to a dental appointment! Ruth was game! As she relayed my message to the teacher there was silence on our end. Mrs. Snyder was quickly explaining how Joseph had become limited in his movement due to an experiment with Sergeant Potter's handcuffs. She ended the phone call by telling Ruth that she'd bring Joseph to the office and explain the situation to his mother.

As we waited for Mrs. Snyder and her handcuffed student to arrive I couldn't stop laughing. *"Boy, this had gone well,"* I thought. But there was a minuscule amount of doubt, *"Would Mrs. Snyder find this as humorous as I did?"* All of this would be at her expense, but surely she'd be relieved to have no angry parent questioning her unusual classroom techniques...I hoped.

I was not disappointed. As Mrs. Snyder rounded the corner into the office with her prisoner in tow I could wait no longer. "Gotcha!" burst from my mouth with a belly laugh. Her eyes and smile grew harmoniously. "I'm going to hurt you!" she promised. Then I unlocked the handcuffs, freeing Joseph from his joyful and extended incarceration.

As the three of us walked back to class I asked Mrs. Snyder what she was thinking when Ruth called. She replied, "I didn't know Joseph's parents, but I was hoping he got his good sense of humor from them and that they wouldn't be upset."

Mrs. Snyder also explained that prior to their long walk to the office she had shared with our class that Joseph's mother was there to pick him up. Everyone had roared, wondering what would happen next!

We all learned lessons that day. Despite the loss of time from class, the students really appreciated the interplay of drama and humor between two teachers. The fact that we adults could publicly play a joke and show good sportsmanship while including the youth was a lesson worth watching. But Joseph had been the real teacher. While Mrs. Snyder and I had feared the worse, he had gone with the flow, enjoying the moment.

15

Hazard Duty

"WILL YOU SIT BESIDE ME AT LUNCH?"

"409, Dispatch."
"Go ahead 409."
"10-10, East Prairie Grade School."
"10-4, 409."

Whenever I get a chance to have lunch with the children I jump at it because it strengthens our relationship and I know the children won't be the only ones learning something. The biggest surprise is that I'm still surprised about what comes out of a seemingly superficial conversation.

Nearly every school lunchroom I've shared with students has had a noise issue. Kids get excited! Talking too loudly is especially a noticeable problem when the children are squeezed tightly together and told to eat quickly. Even the quietest student in class may be an active conversationalist at lunchtime because it's kids' time to talk freely about things they want to discuss. But talking and eating over a school lunch period that sometimes is only twenty minutes long (including waiting in line) is good training if they want to pursue a career in law enforcement—they can learn to eat and run.

I enjoy the lunch periods because I feel the spirit of the children better during these less structured occasions when they are able to interact more personally. *If* I can hear our conversations over the sometimes noisy cafeteria, it also prepares me for the class after lunch. I'll learn who's absent, who's been in trouble and why, and the general mood of the day,

Because of the volume of noise, some schools have tried installing traffic lights. These colored beacons are set to activate at particular sound levels.   The green, or go light, encourages the young people to continue talking at their present volume. A yellow or amber light informs the students the room is getting too noisy, and it's time to use quieter voices. When the red light is electronically tripped it means the mass of students is too loud and that there will be negative consequences. Generally the red light rule dictates no more talking until the lunchroom supervisor permits it, plus there is a fine for the violation...sometimes a delay before going out to recess.

Whether it's a lunchroom traffic light turning red or students not lining up quickly enough, group consequences really are a big part of social learning at school. It's the hope of every teacher that children will use peer pressure in a positive way, beginning with the realization that each person has the ability, if not responsibility, to encourage their classmates to make good decisions.

* * *

I get to sit next to a fourth grade boy who has brought his lunch in a Harry Potter lunch bag. The drawing of the legendary orphan creates questions from some nearby boys.

"Doesn't the lunch bag owner look like Harry?"

"Who's the world's strongest wizard?"

"Sgt. Potter, do you have a child named Harry?"

Then there are the books and the movies. One boy thinks that seeing the movie first has helped him better understand the reading of the book. Another boy says that seeing the movie first ruins the fun of reading the novel because you already know what will happen.

On another day a student again connects my name to Harry Potter. I tell him my dad's name is Harold. He asks if he's magical. I want to use the child's vocabulary so I say "yes," knowing my father is special. I ask the boy about his dad.

"Is he magical?"

He thinks, then replies. "Yes, he can lift me up with one finger!"

Then a scientific experiment occurs before my very eyes. Is the liquid in the thermos, which Mom has packed for her son, water or pop? I'm guessing water. It looks like water. The Harry Potter look-alike is waiting to find out. The little scientist pours it out into a cup. Once he sees the bubbles he has his answer. "It's pop," he declares.

The lunchroom teacher blows her whistle. Was someone speeding? Yes, two girls were running. A verbal warning is issued. But considering the multitude of students eating and talking, at least from my spot at one table, the lunchroom noise is acceptable. We can easily hear each other talking.

Kids raise their hands and the "traffic cop" lunchroom teacher answers their questions. She's doing a great job of monitoring the entire area. Then someone talks too loudly. Were they yelling? Her whistle blows and a boy is easily identified as the culprit. To the bleachers he goes, carrying his tray of food. Isolation is the penalty but it will only be a sentence of a few minutes. Lunchtime is nearly over. Recess can't be far away.

Despite my risky environment it looks like I've made it safely through another lunch period. Sometimes my uniform seems to be a target for flying food from cooperative learning groups doing methodical experiments. There have been exploding oranges, salad dressing launched from child-safety packets, milk erupting from nearby nostrils, and the pouring of pop too close to me. Regardless of my evasive action training and my religious wearing of body armor, these are the risks I accept whenever I sit down at a table full of energetic students. Should I be getting hazard pay?

Hey, I'm also dangerous to sit next to! The other day I was visiting with sixth graders and I was excited to be a part of the conversation. I wanted to jump in when one student asked a question, but I had food in my mouth. It didn't stop me. Out came my food, back onto my plate and all three youngsters saw it. Oh, well! Recovering, I said "I shouldn't be talking with my mouth full."

Not a minute later, one of the students said, "Why do parents tell you not to talk with your mouth full?"

"I'm an example of why!" I tell them. "Besides the risk of choking you can spit out your food at the people you're talking to!"

Knowing and following table manners are just some of the unwritten rules that can help people become successful outside their peer group or economic class. As I take another bite, I'm counting my number of chews, reminding myself to be a better role model.

The traffic light flashes to red. Instinctively the traffic cop responds, blowing her whistle and notifying the entire assembly that it *will* be quiet. She's a disciplinarian and I think it's great! But when she tells the fourth grade that they will have to go back to their regular seating arrangement starting tomorrow I see the dread in the eyes of the students across from me. Something more serious than I can imagine has just occurred. When they are again permitted to talk I learn that for the foreseeable future they will be seated boy-girl-boy-girl. Now that will no doubt lower the decibel level. At this age boys like to sit with boys and girls like to sit with girls. I can't help but wonder what they would talk about now. How will the conversations change? Will the lunchroom be more peaceful? Like it or not, these ten-year olds will have an unstructured lesson in appreciating diversity.

The whistle blows again. A girl is sent to the bleachers for talking too loudly. She goes to an isolated spot. The boy I'm sitting next to is not as happy with the lunchroom monitor as I am. He says with disgust, "She treats everybody like it's her school!" I'm silent, observing, thinking about what he's said. It is her school. She cares. It's obvious to me. But it's his school, too. So I wonder how much cooperation and communication has gone into this lunchroom plan? From my adult perspective it seems much better than last year. Fewer problems. But I'm an adult. I promise myself to continue to observe and listen. Should lunch room behavior be discussed at the next student council meeting? I'll bet they can think of some ideas short of junior noise police. This boy needs to share his recommendations, or at least his perspective. He might also benefit from the concept that when people talk louder so that others can hear them, before long everyone is talking louder to be understood. That makes chaos.

* * *

"Do any of you have chores you do at home?" I ask the second grade students sitting around me in the cafeteria.

"Yes, I get to do the dishes," replies a girl whose napkin is nearly in her apple sauce.

"What do you like about doing them?"

"I get to play in the bubbles."

"That's a great way to have fun," I agree.

"When Mom's not home I get in the bathtub with my swimsuit on and wash the dishes in the bubble bath. That's fun too!"

* * *

"Twenty-two days until I get my braces tightened," a sixth grade girl sitting next to me at lunch informs me. "I can't have bubble gum, taffy, chocolate, or popcorn," she continues.

"Popcorn?" I comment.

"Well, I still eat popcorn because it doesn't get in the braces. Had some at the movies over the weekend."

A friend across the table, also with braces, asks if the popcorn eater will get a retainer after she gets her braces off. Popcorn Girl isn't sure.

From the topic of braces our conversation moves to spelling bees. I discover that each grade is given a spelling test and then the top two spellers are selected to be in the contest that will be held in the gym. Popcorn tells me the name of the two boys who will represent the sixth grade and that her score was one point below theirs.

I find out from Popcorn that she has represented her class every year in counting or spelling until this year.

"Amazing!" I reply.

Then Popcorn says, "I don't care about being in it this year, but I don't know why."

I let her comment hang. She doesn't want to admit she cares or that it hurts that she didn't get what she expected. But I let it pass, wondering later if I should have consoled her loss.

* * *

On another day, after the recent death of a family pet rooster, Hubcap Houdini, I'm looking for a conversation with understanding, like-minded people. "Can anyone tell me a chicken story?" I inquire. I've asked the right students, knowing these girls have raised roosters in their backyards. The more talkative girl, always thoughtful and often smiling, is the first to respond.

"We had a rooster named Rambo. He had spurs this long. He was mean. One day when I was wearing thick socks and sweat pants he pecked my leg and made it bleed! I still have the scar."

"Bleeding!" I respond.

Then she reaches towards her pants and I can tell that she knows the exact location of that former battle field injury. She concludes that after her little brother was attacked by Rambo, her dad got rid of the overly aggressive bird. I didn't ask if he was dinner.

* * *

Recess is nearly upon us and I still have food on my plate. I look around and do a quick survey of others. Am I eating at an elderly pace? The plastic trays sitting before the students are in different states of readiness for the nearby trash cans. Most are nearly empty. Some show the results of curiosity like the color theory project performed by two boys when salad dressing and ketchup were mixed. A few trays have nearly all the original servings of food remaining. *"Why aren't these kids eating?"* I ask myself.

* * *

At a recent lunch, sitting across from three fourth grade students, the one boy, Julian, tells me he wants to be a sheriff's deputy when he's an adult. He quickly gets my attention because I'm more used to the public using the term "police officer" to describe any and all law enforcement personnel.

Someone will be asking me if I know a friend of theirs who's a police officer. I'll ask if they know what department they're on and they aren't sure if he works for the city as a police officer, for the county as a deputy sheriff or for the state as a highway patrol officer. Sometimes we learn later that the individual was a correctional guard at the prison or a private security officer. Do all uniforms look alike? For many people they do.

It's understandable and fair that we all get bunched together with general labels. Not making those distinctions is common for anyone outside or removed from the business. For years I've asked for a "Kleenex"® when really all I've wanted is a facial tissue. The expression "police officer" is a generic term applying to a person professionally trained and entrusted by a government (city, county, province, state, federal) to maintain public peace and order, enforcement of laws, and the prevention and detection of crime.[19]

Over our lunch together Julian tells me of his plans to go to college and then to become a sheriff's deputy. Margo explains that she is prepared for many years of study in school in order to become a doctor. Brandy isn't sure what she wants to do. I tell her that's sure okay since she's only a fourth grader! Then I ask her what she likes to do and her body comes alive, eyes lighting up, matching her growing smile. "Shopping!" she exclaims.

"Maybe you'll be a personal shopper. Have you heard of that?"

"No."

"They're people who get hired to purchase

items for others who don't have the time or talent. Personal shoppers are experts on shopping. They give advice. For example, if someone wants to buy an outfit but they don't have an idea what to buy, this person can give advice and recommendations once they learn the occasion where it's to be worn."

"Hmmm...that sounds interesting," she replies.

"There's another job that pays people to shop, but I don't think you get as much time to really get involved in the creativity of styles, matching clothing and comparing prices. Have you ever heard of a secret or mystery shopper?"

"No."

"Companies hire people to go shopping in order to discover how welcoming and professional their employees are at their stores. They learn if the sales clerk greeted them and if they were able to answer their questions about the merchandise. The secret or undercover shopper might even learn and later report that the sales clerk was rude to them. Those are things management wants to know so they can improve training."

"Do the secret shoppers get to keep the things they buy?"

"No, I don't think so. I guess that wouldn't be as much fun then, would it?"

"Well, I might want to be a doctor like Margo."

"If you were a doctor then with your income you could do a lot of your own shopping and keep the merchandise. I see most everyone else is lining up. We better stop talking and clean our trays."

"Okay."

After I toss my silverware in the soapy water and add my tray to the growing stack, I'm stopped by two third grade boys. They report to me that Julian was calling them bad names just before I sat down at the table. I get details. Then I find Julian who is getting ready, along with his class, for recess.

I approach him and ask him if I can speak with him. We move away from the others far enough for privacy. I get down on the floor, cross my legs in a sitting position. He follows me to the floor.

"Julian, I'm glad to hear that you want to be a deputy sheriff. Now that I know that's a dream of yours I want to help you achieve your goal. I've been told by some students about the way you curse at them."

"I don't...."

"Hold on. Let me finish. I'm not mad at you. You're not in trouble. I'm just letting you know that in order to become a deputy sheriff you need to respect yourself and to respect others. I'm just letting you know because I want to help you out."

"They say my mother's fat."

"Julian, your teacher has told me that you're making fantastic progress this year on getting along better with your classmates. Keep up the good work. I know it can be hard, but I have a lot of confidence in you. You're always polite around me and that's the kind of behavior that will help you become a deputy sheriff."

"They say my mother's fat."

"Yes, I know, and you say their mothers are fat. That isn't solving the problem. As strong and smart as you are you can do a better job of working this out and showing respect. I know you have teachers and counselors that help you and that they're teaching you skills. They tell me you're continuing to do better. Keep up the good work. Don't let a couple of third grade boys pull you down. Remember, you're not in trouble. I'm only telling you this because now that I know you want to be one of us I feel like I need to let you in on how to become a deputy sheriff. You can do it."

Julian is silent. I haven't given him an opportunity to vent, deny the charges or to tell me his side of the story. Instead, I've given him a lecture I was trying to disguise as a helping hand. He has to decide if at recess he will be mad or not. I hope that because of our good relationship, at some point he might think about what I've said. Will my brief comments reinforce the valuable advice he's been receiving from other teachers and support staff?

Like most days after lunch I walk the children to recess. On this particular day, before Julian and I reach the playground, walking through the hallway, I'm asked a question from behind: "Sgt. Potter, what are you playing at recess?"

My response is immediate. "Football! Can Julian and I be on the same team?"

16

KID TIME

"ARE YOU PLAYING AT RECESS?"

"What's your favorite class at school?"
"Lunch and recess."
"Me, too."

———

There's a big difference between "going to" and "playing at" recess.

"Sgt. Potter, are you playing at recess?" is an invitation to a child's world of fun. So far this semester it's mostly been foursquare, kickball, soccer, and tether ball. Football and basketball can't be far behind. With the younger kids tag is still a favorite. I've seen sixth grade students having fun with this childish game while being very competitive. They might complain about running track in P.E. yet burn more calories just playing with friends at recess.

Recess is a great way for me to get to know my students. One game played together can make a huge difference in class participation, because there's been a new connection between us. Now I admire Jessica or Jeremiah for their athletic skills and tell them so. I quickly discover if the class practices good sportsmanship. Who argues a call when they think they're right? Who plays by the rules? Who cheats? And who compliments their competitor for a good game whether they win or lose? Recess is where I discover a whole new level of involvement among the students. Outside the classroom is where I build the strength of my teaching.[20]

If I'm given the choice between playing a sport or talking, football and basketball usually win out. Sometimes it's a challenge for me to slow down, to make myself available for a conversation. But, my aches and injuries come easily enough and before you know it conversations are more appealing. After about fifteen consecutive games of tether ball one recess I was feeling pretty good until I woke up the next day with a sore shoulder, wondering if I'd been in a car wreck during the night. Another day I sprained an ankle playing basketball during an indoor recess with far too many players on the small court. After a visit to my local doctor I was on crutches for a week. It was surprising how many people assumed I had been injured in a fight with a criminal. They wanted an exciting story about my struggle with a bad guy, but instead they heard my version of going up for a rebound from a fifth grader and landing on the side of my foot. How boring!

You know you're getting older when, as you leave for work, your wife warns you to be careful and to not act like a kid at recess. It's also an example of how far I've traveled since working patrol. Back then "be careful out there" was a reference to the criminal element, not a sports injury at grade school recess.

I continue to learn that some students prefer talking more than playing and to remember to make time for them too. If it weren't for me being at recess Herb might have never told me about his grandfather.

"Officer Potter, my grandfather died. He was 'crustafied' because it was cheaper than being buried."

At another recess I learned that a student had a new member in her family. The thirteen-year old told me of a new baby sister born after her mother had a c-section and that the baby had "a little butt." I remarked, "For a baby that's one-day old, everything's little." In our conversation I realized that this girl, who rarely paid attention in science class was telling me she'd held a newborn baby for two hours, changed a diaper, and noticed the blood from where the umbilical cord was cut.

The younger kids at recess will sometimes play imaginary games. When I watch, I learn volumes. They'll play fort, jail or family.

One recess a girl named Diana was pretending to be the mother in a family. During her acting she slapped a younger girl hard in the face for "refusing to watch the kids at home."

Two years later I bumped into that same girl and her mother at the mall. I learned from the young teen that days earlier she had been taken to the emergency room after her father had hit her in the head. He was arrested for domestic violence. I recalled her previous playground behavior. It made me wonder just how much the pretending that children do at school is actually mimicking behavior at home. If children are acting out violence then where are they learning the script? Is it from the media, an active imagination or from real life?

Watching the way kids play can alert us to all kinds of possibilities.

Although recess is designed to let the students blow off steam, sometimes they blow up. A game of fun may turn violent. Some students, especially the very competitive ones, don't like to lose at anything. That attitude may be the foundation for success or it may lead to arguments that push the limits. I was at one recess where a boy, Chris, didn't let the other smaller boy, Sean, get up off the ground quickly enough. A couple of minutes later, immediately after recess, Sean followed Chris into the teacherless classroom, made a fist and slugged his target squarely in the face. Despite our classroom lessons on making good decisions, Sean, still upset at being held down, had acted out his fist full of frustrations. We wondered if his actions were partially due to the dramatic divorce of his parents and the tumultuous example they were setting for him on handling conflict. Or, his response might have been programmed behavior, expected by parents who teach their children that earning someone's respect means never walking away from a fight unfinished. Whatever Sean's reasons, he was suspended from school.

On extremely cold or wet days the children might stay inside. They'll either be sent to the gymnasium to play, to their classroom or even the hallway. This indoor recess can mean an assortment of activities, including board games. I'm always looking for a good chess match, but sometimes I'll get an opportunity to learn a new game.

The whole idea of recess, the chance to not have to do something, is quite a concept.

It's the adults letting the kids relax, to make choices about what they want to do. It's a moment of freedom. This break in the day is so important to the children. Understandably, it's used as leverage by the teachers. A class of kids can easily lose two minutes of recess even though collectively a majority of them have been behaving. In recent years the entire group is punished less often, but I can certainly appreciate the motivation and the frustration that creates blanket punishments. I've done it despite remembering how unfair I thought it was when I was a student. When individuals can be identified for displaying irresponsible or inappropriate behavior then they, not everyone, deserve a consequence.

Speaking of consequences, once I got in trouble at a recess for not knowing the playground rules! Brittany and Taylor were on one side of the teeter-totter and I was on the other. Our weight was virtually balanced. I had the sensation of my childhood as I occasionally, just for a second, held the girls up in the air then let it bounce with a thud. This was fun I'd forgotten after so many years! Then, it happened. I felt like I was back in grade school even though I was a uniformed, armed, adult. The playground teacher looked over at us, directed her full attention at me, and said in her most authoritarian voice: "Only two on the teeter-totter at a time." I'd been caught breaking the rules! As I walked off she nailed me again. Like a laser beam to my back, she directed each word with incredible focused power: "You know where the office is!" Even though my long time colleague and friend was in jest I felt for all the world like I was little Jimmy Potter back in the third grade.

At another school's recess I was talking to a couple of the teachers when I noticed the flag football game had abruptly stopped. Everyone was looking south, out of our sight, beyond the wing of the building.

"I wonder what's going on," I said; then I went to investigate.

"Is anyone hurt?" I asked, then learned that Darius had had his pants fall down when someone grabbed his flag. Checking around, I saw a boy bent over crying.

"Go play the game. I'll talk with him," I told a small group of his friends, allowing some privacy for the star subject. I knelt down and waited.

"What happened? Are you all right?"

Stammering, he told me, "I'm embarrassed."

I observed the broken snaps on his break away basketball pants. "Do you have any gym shorts here at school that you can put on under them?"

"Uh-huh," he mumbled.

"You can change into them but first you'll need to be able to go back out to your classmates and laugh about this." He was obviously not ready for that yet. I explained that having someone's pants accidentally come down is funny to see. "Your classmates weren't laughing at you, but they were laughing at what happened. You need to be able to laugh, too." I didn't think he was buying it so I decided to just get him to think about something else. "Stand up and do what I do." Then I touched my head with one hand and rubbed my stomach with the other. He reluctantly played along until his anxiety relaxed. After awhile I put my arm around his shoulder and we walked back to the playground where I explained the circumstances to his teacher.

Darius asked her if he could change into his gym shorts. His teacher was ready to tell him about her most embarrassing moment. I thought of the vicious canine that had jumped into my patrol car. We all had a story. Maybe, I thought, Darius could use this embarrassing crisis when he was older, but first he needed to survive the day.

* * *

Children need time to explore and be creative. This can happen at recess.

I meet the sweetest kids at school. There was one girl, Lauren, who came up to talk to me in the lunchroom. Alert to her surroundings she wanted to find out what I was doing in school.

"Are you a real police man? Are you Kevin's grandfather? My grandfather is a police officer in Oklahoma. I have a friend who's afraid of police officers. Will you meet her?"

She wanted to introduce me to everyone! *"Wow!"* I thought. *"She's going places! What will she be doing as an adult?"*

Before the meal was over, Lauren, smiling, found me again. "Will you be going out to the playground after lunch?"

I'd thought about it and with that invitation it was a sure thing. Once outside I saw that the children had started their internal engines. They were having all the fun they wanted without playing on any of the playground equipment. They were like cats with a paper bag, cardboard

172 *Cop in the Classroom*

box or captured mouse. It didn't take much for them to be cheaply entertained.

Most of the kids were busily digging in the dirt beneath an old cottonwood tree. They used sticks the length of clothespins, like hand trowels at an archeological site. I watched the orderly excavation going on around one of its sizeable roots. The scene reminded me of my own summer spent on hands and knees at an archeological dig in Winchester, England, where I eagerly searched for Roman coins and royal jewels.

But back in the USA, this busy group of children was getting early training for future hobbies or careers. They held a clear and common goal, a mission: Dig up this tree!

In a moment of adulthood and questionable humor I said, "Hope the tree doesn't fall over if you pull up that root." A few heads looked up at me, wondered if I was a danger to their project, then they decided I was harmless and could be ignored.

Nearby, two sisters were playing school on the sidewalk. The smaller one, seven-years old, had a book with math problems. I soon learned firsthand that she had extensive skills in addition and subtraction. How much were her math skills part of her identity?

Lauren and I were talking among a small group of girls when I discovered that I knew her mother. I told the gregarious girl, "Are you sure you're her daughter?"

She replied insistently, "I came from her stomach!"

When I was asked by Lauren if I'd go meet another friend, a boy who was occupied putting leaves and pebbles down a small opening in a man hole cover, I moved too quickly. As I rose and turned my body I brought my bony elbow up as though I were a basketball player protecting the ball from aggressive opponents. Smack! I hit a little girl, Hannah, squarely in the eye. She wasn't crying, but she was primed. I immediately apologized, told her it was my fault and wondered if she was going to break into tears. Her face resembled a dam, holding back a good howl. I let the playground teacher know that later on the little girl might require an ice pack. Boy, was I relieved that I hadn't injured the girl who was afraid of police officers!

At the end of the recess I said goodbye to Lauren and Hannah. The latter was smiling despite a red mark by her eye the perfect size of my elbow.

* * *

I still vividly remember the excitement of exploration, shared with me at a spring recess.

"Officer Potter! Officer Potter!" Two boys, both about eight-years old come running up to me as I join the outdoor recess. They each have something in their closed hands and are tremendously excited! I'm wondering what unfortunate insect has been captured today.

"Officer Potter, look at these rocks!" they blurt out simultaneously.

"Nice!" I exaggerate, but their enthusiasm is catchy. Soon I'm appreciating the guidance of these young scientists and I'm eager to learn.

The smallest boy is the most animated. Voice inflection is not a problem as he recalls his father's comments about rocks, "My dad says that some rocks we find might be valuable." Then, explaining his own belief: "Some people say that they aren't worth anything because they're not shiny, but if you break them, some rocks are shiny on the inside."

I can't help myself. I lick my finger and wet one of the pebbles. It sparkles for a few moments and we look at it in the sun.

I'm thankful for them reminding me of my playground days of discovery in the dirt. I, too, would imagine that one of the rocks I examined was not pyrite, or fool's gold, but in fact was the real thing and that I was suddenly rich.

"There are scientists that study rocks. Do you know what they're called?" I'm questioned.

"Geologists," I answer and the boys seem surprised.

"This is shale and this one is granite," I'm informed.

The teacher's whistle blows and the boys, a good pound heavier than before recess, are in motion to line up with their classmates. The smallest boy has bulging pockets. His partner carries a dirty white sock laden with his own prized playground possessions...gems to him. Each specimen is spectacular, reminding me of the old saying, "Beauty is in the eye of the beholder."

When the students get settled in their classroom will their teacher marvel at the growing collection of rocks from stuffed pockets and soiled socks or will she discourage the practice? Listening to the enthusiasm of these two boys, I'm guessing she's a supporter, if not an instigator of this learning activity. I'm betting that this educator is a motivator, not a persecutor or prosecutor of young geologists.

17

Discipline or Abuse

"WHAT IF MY STEP-DAD HITS MY BROTHER WITH A BOARD?"

"He who spares the rod hates his son, but he who loves him is diligent to discipline him."
—Proverbs 13:24[21]

Sophia is in trouble at school because of a fight at recess. Like many conflicts it began with name calling, progressed to pushing, and culminated with hitting. We call that going up the conflict escalator. The push or shove she received was nothing compared to the very personal biting words from the younger and smaller girl. But both these girls can be as sweet as they are mean. On any given day they might be mortal enemies *or* close friends. I wonder how they can change from one to the other so quickly. Then I recall how my sister, Mary, and I could fight about anything, everything, and nothing every day after school for a year-and-a-half when we were their ages of eleven and twelve. These girls are in that same strange stage of immaturity Mary and I experienced so long ago in an age called adolescence!

I know the girl I'm facing across the table in the principal's office is dealing with stressors beyond my experience. She has challenges at home with her step-father, whom I see at church. He works on a production line on a night shift in the food industry. I've heard rumors that he's got a nasty temper.

I really don't know her step-father, but I've seen him and his family on occasion at church over the last couple of years. We greet one another in the parking lot and in the sanctuary. He drives a Ford pickup with a bumper sticker on the rear window that announces, "God is my Co-pilot." Strange as it may seem, I don't recall if I've ever heard his first name. Everyone calls him by his nickname, "Wheels." What I'm not clear about is if his moniker is from his love of driving extra-large and powerful trucks with oversize tires or from his shiny, chrome, non-motorized wheelchair which sports a bumper sticker boasting, "This vehicle insured by Smith & Wesson." On more than one occasion I've observed members at church take a second look at the message on this bumper sticker. It definitely makes people think.

Sophia and I are sitting by ourselves across from each other in the principal's office and I simply ask her to tell me why she's here. My adult voice is clear but soft. I want her to know that in spite of my law enforcement uniform, and knowing her step-dad, I'm not planning on giving her another lecture, advice or another consequence. Well, maybe a little advice.

"I'm here to hear your side of the story," I state.

"What do you mean?" Sophia questions.

"You're in the principal's office and you're not allowed back in class. I've been told that you were fighting on the playground. The other girl's not here. You are. Do you want to tell me what it was all about?"

"Okay. One of my best friends, Taylor, told me that Helen told her that the only boys who liked me were losers who couldn't get anyone pretty or nice to go out with them. After lunch when I was walking with Patricia, we saw Helen so I told her to mind her own business. A minute later Helen came back and told me that she heard the boy I liked was stupid and that if he liked me that was proof enough of how ignorant he really must be. I told her to get away or else she'd be sorry she had such a big mouth. Then she pushed me and I pushed her back. That's all."

"When the teacher responded to the pushing that was going on, how did you handle that? I heard that you were rude to her," I inquire.

"I didn't hear what she said to me the first time. Then she got mad at me because I didn't come with her and she started shouting at me. I yelled back. Then she told me to go to the office. That's it."

"It sounds to me as though you and Helen are really angry at one another. Would you like me to help arrange a sit-down with her so you two can talk this out? Or do you want me to leave it alone?"

"We may spend Friday night together at her house. She's seeing if I can come over. We're friends again."

Confused, I ask, "Didn't the fight just happen?"

"It was yesterday. We talked on the phone last night."

Amazed and befuddled, I said, "It sounds like you and Helen have taken care of one problem. What about you and Miss Pegenkoff? Have the two of you worked things out?"

"Sorta. We're talking."

"Sophia, I know that words can really hurt you. Remember that you're pretty, you can be nice and you're smart. When anyone says things to try to hurt another person it's really an indication about how they're feeling about themselves. Mean words are spoken when someone is already feeling mean. They're unhappy."

"I know about mean words. I hear them at home from my step-dad all the time. He'll tell me and my older brother, Henry, that we aren't much to look at and that if we don't obey him we'll roast in hell. Wheels also tells Henry that someday the cops will take him away in a straight jacket and that he'll end up in a mental institution."

"Whoa! That's not healthy talking."

"Wheels says my brother needs counseling. Wheels needs the counseling, not my brother."

"Maybe they both do. Maybe we all do."

"Henry gets hit almost every day by Wheels for doing something wrong. He uses a board on his behind."

"A board or a paddle? What does it look like?"

"It's about this long," explains Sophia as she holds out two hands about two feet apart. "He carries it with him all the time on the back of his wheel chair. On one side of the board he's written 'PEACE' with a marker and on the other side 'WAR'. "

"I've seen it! I just didn't know for sure what he used it for."

"He uses it to reach things, hit things...for anything. He always has it with him."

"When he hits Henry, does he always hit him on his behind? Do you watch?"

"Oh yeah, I see it all the time. On his rear end. But he hasn't swatted me for years."

As I rearrange a pencil already lying on the table separating us I use it as a prop. "There's a difference between parents disciplining a child and abusing a child. Sometimes it's not clear to law enforcement officers because the hitting happens in the home, hidden from the public. Other times it's not easy to tell the difference because not everyone working in the law interprets the law the same way. If the pencil here is the law there are times that it's hard to tell if a parent has gone over the line of the law to a crime of abuse. Parents are allowed to spank their children, even paddle them to discipline them, but the parent needs to be in control and not hit too hard."

"Henry gets hit almost every day after school. Wheels says that God's law in Proverbs tells him to beat us to deliver our souls from hell, and that the United States Constitution also gives him the right."

"What does Henry do that causes Wheels to hit him?"

"Since Wheels works from six at night until six in the morning he's still trying to sleep when

we get home. We each go to our rooms and try
to be quiet. But if we make any noise Wheels
will get mad. Henry also gets into fights with
kids at school and for arguing with teachers.
Mom says Wheels hits Henry because he's tired.
I think she's scared of him too."

"Is she home when Henry gets hit?"

"A lot of the time."

"Henry and I have a name we call Wheels, but
he doesn't know about it. It's our little secret
joke. We call him 'Squeaky' because when he
tries to sneak outside our bedroom doors we
can hear his wheelchair squeaking. No one else
can hear it except the two of us. You won't tell
him will you?"

"Oh, no."

"I don't want Wheels to have to leave our house.
He's nice sometimes and mean sometimes. I
want us to have a father that doesn't move away.
I just don't like to be scared of him or for him
to hit Henry so much. We should have a father
while we're growing up...shouldn't we?"

"Let me do some checking with people smarter
than I am. I know there's family counseling
available for working out problems between
family members and learning coping skills. It's
called family preservation.

A week later....

I wonder about Sophia and Henry. Are they
all right? What has happened in their household
over the last week?   I haven't seen Wheels at
church. He's got to know I jumped into his
business. I can't help it. I'm an advocate for
children. Were there consequences for Sophia
talking to me at school? I hope everything is
okay, but I know that she might be withdrawn

and mad at me if things got intimidating or violent. I did what I had to do, but she may not see it that way, and if things got ugly at home I wouldn't blame her for a second for holding me responsible! That's okay. It's part of my job.

I'm sitting with our class of students at the lunch table, a couple of students down and across from Sophia and she says to me, "I got my stuff back."

It's not the first time nor the last time that I'm confused. "What stuff back?"

"In my room."

"Huh?" I mumble.

"I got all my stuff back for my room, my CD player and TV. We all went shopping and Wheels even replaced my TV set that he ripped out of the wall. The lady came and talked to me and I thought Wheels would be angry, but he wasn't. He said I was understanding and reasonable."

"Yes! I'm happy for you! Sometimes things get worse before they get better. It was brave of you to tell me that there was a problem at home. You took a big risk. Congratulations!"

"He threw away the board! He and Mom had a two hour talk in their room about everything. I finally got hungry, asked when they were coming out, and said 'When are we going to eat?' Mom told me to fix something myself. I don't know if Mom told Wheels we would leave if things didn't change, but we all went shopping for clothes and things are better. I've got all my stuff back. Henry was going to get his stuff back, but he's still getting into trouble at school. Wheels said Henry will get his stuff back gradually. We're planning a trip to Colorado this summer, but Henry won't get to go if he doesn't stop getting into trouble. Wheels said they might have to find him a boot camp to be at while we're away. He said it's not fair for Henry to go on a vacation if he's going to spoil it for everyone else."

Four days later....

The honeymoon period is over. Sophia sees me and tells me, "Wheels left two nights ago after yelling at Henry and me. We don't even know what set him off. He told my mom he's tired of being overridden by me and my brother."

"Has he been back?"

"No, but he called last night. I think he might be back tonight. I'm not sure."

"How do you feel about that?" I continue.

Then I hear the silence. Either Sophia's not sure how she feels or she wants to tell me whatever she thinks I want to hear. She may not realize that the right answer is whatever she's feeling.

Appearing to me as though she's in a state of numbness she slowly answers, "I don't feel anything...I don't know...it doesn't matter to me."

Later, in the lunch line....

"Do you know what a point system is?" I'm asked as the class of students prepares for the lunch line. It's Sophia. She could write a book on introductory sentences, hooks or grabbers. I'm listening.

It seems that her first question usually requires some clarification so I ask, "A point system for what?"

"For me and my brother to determine if we have privileges to do things at the end of the week."

"Do you gain or lose points?" I ask.

"We start each day with zero points. If we earn

a hundred points in a day then we get privileges. Right now I have forty points that I earned by getting up this morning without my mom waking me up. To get more points I also need to get ready on my own. My brother only got five points this morning because he didn't set his own alarm clock and she had to wake him up."

"This system sounds good. This can be to your benefit and help you."

"Henry has lost points on his attitude."

"Who decides if you lose points?"

"Mom."

"Can I get a copy of the point system? It really sounds like an excellent idea."

"Mom has it on her computer. I'll get you a copy."

A month later....

"Henry got paddled over the weekend by my step-dad," Sophia announces to me in her always a statement—never a greeting—welcoming way.

"What did he use?" I reply.

"A board. It's got words on it."

"I thought he threw that away!" I said, recalling the earlier conversation.

"It was lost, but he found it. After Henry got paddled my mom and step-dad started arguing. Wheels got mad, threw the paddle down. It hit the couch and then bounced and hit mom. It was an accident. Then he said he was gone, out of there. He took his truck and drove it down the block into a field. I walked down there later and he was sleeping in the front seat. I never know when Wheels will be home and when he's home I don't know which Wheels he'll be. We should have a father while we're growing up... shouldn't we?"

18

Boxing or Bullying

"IF YOU HAD IT TO DO OVER AGAIN WOULD YOU STILL HIT HER?"

"What if you played basketball using the rules of football?" I asked.

"I'd get thrown out of the game!" she replied.

"Exactly! The same is true if you use the survival rules of your neighborhood at school. You get into big trouble."[22]

———————

I couldn't believe what I was hearing! Suanna had punched a classmate for harassing her. How could this be? The Suanna I knew was every teacher's ideal student. She was actively involved in class discussions, intelligent, on task, and a person who spoke from her experience and from her heart. Is this the same person who would deck someone?

Boy, I would get to the bottom of this and soon. I'd seek out the teacher, the principal and Suanna. Despite my partiality towards Suanna, I would be fair to the circumstances. Had she physically assaulted another student for verbally harassing her? If so, this appeared to be out of character—an over reaction. What was the rest of the story? I was hoping I could be a part of the solution.

Before learning the details of the "harassment" I could guess it had to do with one of two things: Suanna's physical appearance or her cultural identity. Throughout her short life, long before I knew her, she was repeatedly a natural target from the insecure who grasped at others to pull them down to their chaotic level. Suanna's father was supposedly a full-blooded American Indian and mother was Caucasian. Suanna was born not dark or light, not bronze, but with an absence of all color. In what seemed inexplicable, she was born albino, most rare in nature.

Suanna had been at the school less than two years, but her biological and cultural circumstances had made her story well known in and out of the teacher's lounge. Teachers would marvel that her mother was recognized statewide in the medical community as a leading geneticist and her father pursued an interesting combination of successful businesses—car repair and Appaloosa horse breeding.

Both Suanna's grade school teachers, this year's and last, continually remarked that they had learned more about Native American traditions through her reports and projects than they had in four years of college courses. Suanna, it seemed, was a favorite, not just to me, but of educators who had a love of learning even as their passion for teaching was challenged every day by increasingly greater demands to "teach to the test."

"No," the secretary told me, "Principal Allison is not available. He is at a meeting and won't be back until late in the school day."

"Yes," the recess duty teacher explained, "yesterday Suanna had punched a classmate and it was a serious punch. Suanna had wound up and hit the bigger girl, Terri, on the jaw which had knocked the known bully to her knees. It was either a fight or an attack, depending on how you looked at it, that had occurred after lunch, near the doorway leading to the playground. Of course, there were varying details from the witnesses interviewed, but surprisingly, both the sixth grade students directly involved agreed that words had led to the physical altercation."

"What did Terri say that caused Suanna to go off?" I asked the teacher.

"According to Suanna, Terri was making fun of her and said something about how Suanna couldn't go out because of the snow. That if she took her clothes off she'd disappear like a snowflake in a snowstorm and nobody could find her. The comments about Suanna's lack of pigmentation were obviously meant to hurt and stir her up. I wouldn't think she'd go so far as to hit Terri in the face. And Suanna, of all people...exploding!"

"Did Terri hit her back?" I continued.

"No. Didn't have a chance. The fight was over before it started. Other students nearby agreed that it was a full fisted punch that knocked Terri to her knees. Now, that must have been a punch! I thought that only happened in boxing matches and soap opera wrestling. I'd have bet it was impossible from a twelve-year-old girl. Terri's a big kid and we know she's been in a fight or two. I'm surprised that Suanna would stand up to Terri. By the way, Terrible Terri seems to be okay, but the former Sweet Suanna may have broken her hand! That's what happens when you hit bone to bone. Something's gotta' give."

"What happened to the girls? Was Suanna suspended? How about Terri?" I continued.

"The only consequence for Terri teasing Suanna was getting hit. She's being viewed as the victim here rather than the bully. Suanna's the one, rightly so, in trouble. I mean, I like her but she never told me that Terri was making fun of her and I was on recess duty. She got off lightly. Yesterday afternoon her mother was called at work and told to come pick her up. When she arrived, Suanna was in Mr. Allison's office with her hand wrapped in an ice pack. I haven't heard what was said, but Suanna was taken to the Medical Center for x-rays. She's back in school today. She got a three-day ISS (in school suspension) rather than any OSS (out of school) time. Had it been a boy you know he would have been home for a week!"

"Maybe, but she's never been in a fight before at school, has she? How did Terri's parents take this? Are they upset?"

"Fortunately for Suanna they didn't make a big deal out of it. They said 'Terri probably got what she deserved for her big mouth.' Terri seems fine. The only thing bruised is her ego."

"Would it be all right for me to speak with Suanna?" I asked.

"Sure. She's in the back room of the library. I'm glad you're concerned. Let me know what you find out. I haven't talked with her since yesterday, but I did prepare her assignments and sent them down with her books."

"Thanks. I'm going to go find her," I said.

* * *

"Hello Suanna. How are you?"

"Okay."

"I'm glad to see you. What happened? Why are you here?"

"I got in a fight yesterday."

"It looks like it! What happened to your hand? Is it broken?"

"The doctor said it's a hairline fracture. It's wrapped up for protection."

"So, do you have time to talk with me? I'd like to learn more about what caused the fight and to see if I can be of any help?"

"I've got plenty of time. Yeah, I'll talk with you, but I don't see how you can help."

"Now, I'm not investigating this as a crime, but sometimes people are charged with battery when they hit someone else, unless it's clearly self defense. The school wants to handle this without a police report. I'm here to see if I can understand what happened. You never know, I might have a good idea."

"If you talk to Terri she'll tell you that she and her friends were just joking around."

"I'm not talking to her right now. I'm listening to your side of the story."

"I don't think you or any adult can understand why I hit her."

"Give me a try," I encouraged.

"You wouldn't understand. It's just the way it is. You just can't know what it's like to be a kid that's picked on every day."

"You're right." I could only agree. "I don't know what it's like to be picked on every day."

"You're a police officer. You don't get picked

on and even if you got made fun of when you were my age, you can't remember what it was like."

"Hmmm...it was a long time ago."

"I like being with my friends at school and learning new things, but I don't like rude people messing with me.   How do I change that?   I can't."

Agreeing with her comments about rude people, I said, "We do have some things in common.   If only everyone else would be like you and me, life would be so much easier!"

"See, I know you're trying to be funny, but every day I come to school I get made fun of by a group of girls.   And nothing ever happens to them."

"I was just realizing how difficult it is to get people to change.   But surely in school the teachers have a lot of control over students who misbehave."

"That's what most people think, but the teachers are busy teaching lessons.   Our class has been a real problem for them since I came here in the fifth grade.   Things haven't got any better, only worse."

"Do the teacher's know you get made fun of?"

"They have to know Terri's rude because she's even rude to them!   Usually when she picks on me it's either in the hallway, when the teacher's out of the room, or at recess.   It happens everywhere, especially on the bus. That's the way my school day begins and the way it ends."

"Do the teachers know how bad it is for you?"

"No.   Only my best friend, Holly, and my parents know."

"Thanks for telling me. I didn't know it was so prevalent...so constant. Do you ever get relief from this, to just relax or have some fun?"

"At home and when I'm with Holly! I have the best parents. They understand me, well... usually. But my mom's not too happy about this fight. She's disappointed in me for hitting Terri. She doesn't know what to do with me, so I'm grounded. That includes talking on the phone. I haven't been able to speak with Holly since my mom took me to the doctor's office yesterday."

"What about your dad? How's he handling this?"

"He and Mom don't agree on what I should do. They try to tell me how to respond to people who make fun of me, but then they each tell me something different to do. Mom always thinks I should ignore them. Dad thinks that Terri got what she deserved, but he said it would have been better to have waited for her to touch me, then I would have been within my legal rights."

"That's interesting."

"I love my mom, but my dad's the one I can talk to about anything. He always takes the time to listen and understand what I need, and lately that seems like every day after school. I'm glad he works at home."

"You're fortunate to have caring parents that are available. Sometimes it's difficult to know what the best response should be to difficult situations. I don't know for sure how I would have handled Terri. I might have tried ignoring her or avoiding her. I can't imagine hitting her, especially at school!"

"Believe me when I tell you I've ignored mean

comments in school since third grade and I do try to avoid certain people. It's kind of impossible to pretend your classmates aren't around when you have to sit next to them all day."

"Yes, I'll bet that's hard."

"I didn't know I was going to hit her until I hit her. Now I'm told I have an anger problem! Hello? Yes, I'm angry for being made fun of! Who wouldn't be? How about Terri? Does anyone notice she's my problem? Why doesn't someone fix her?"

"I'll be talking to Terri later. She's your test. We all get tested and we all have our limits."

"Now you sound like my dad. He says anyone can be pushed to their limit."

"Yes, that's true. But I'm thinking about you feeling good about yourself after losing control. It's difficult to feel good about yourself when you're being insulted, but it's nearly impossible to feel good about yourself when you're out of control. How do you feel about what you did? Would you do anything differently in a similar situation if it happened tomorrow?"

"It won't happen for at least two more days, because we won't see each other. I'm in this room all day, including for lunch. My mom's dropping me off on her way to work and my dad's picking me up after school. But...But...."

"But what?"

"I know if I tell you this you'll think I deserve being punished but...I'm glad I hit Terri."

"Because? Because she deserved it?"

"Because she'll think twice before picking on me again. So will her friends. My parents tell me I can't be around adults all the time to protect me, that I need to solve my own problems."

"You need to solve your own problems without creating other problems. Remember that the way you solve problems on the street doesn't always work when you're at school or a job. What do the principal and the teachers tell you to do if you're being bothered by someone?"

"To t-e-l-l a teacher."

"Have you tried that?"

"Yes, yes and yes. But I can't do it all the time. It just doesn't work that way. It can make things worse. I knew you wouldn't understand... you all think alike."

"Wait a minute. So, telling a teacher doesn't work and now hitting is your answer?"

"I'm not saying I'll do it again. I'm just saying the kids will think about what I can do to them rather than what they can do to me."

"So, you're willing to accept the consequences?"

"I'm not happy about it. My parents aren't either. But, yes, I'm accepting the punishment for hitting Terri. Being here in the library isn't bad. Besides, after all these years, I'm glad I'm finally getting to use some of my self-defense skills. My dad's taught me how to box since I was little."

"Now, Suanna, I don't mean to argue with you, but I'm trying to give you another look at what you're saying. You've told me that you're sick and tired of being made fun of and that teachers don't or can't protect you all the time."

"Yep. That's what happens."

"Now you're telling me that what you call self-defense, hitting someone that verbally attacks you, is the answer?"

"You look at it like a police officer...or a lawyer. I look at it after being pushed around for so long. No, I didn't get hit first, but if I would have talked back to Terri she would have hit me. Can't you see it my way? I think in social studies, when we talked about Iraq, the teacher called that a 'preemptive strike'."

"Okay. You're saying that you need to stand up for yourself because no one else is. You had to hit her to let her know to back off, that she better watch out or else it might happen again, that you aren't going to take the verbal trash talk anymore. Plus, you're not sorry for what you did and you're willing to accept the consequences from school and from home."

"Now you've got it. Except, I may never hit her or anyone again, except my dad...in boxing. It's not like I'm going to go around attacking people the way Terri does."

"Is there a way for you to use your boxing skills on a team outside of school? You could be recognized for your talent. Then you could wear padded gloves to protect your hands and to keep from injuring others. Tell me this, what kind of rules do you follow when you box with your dad? Are you under control when you hit him? Are there rules or boundaries about getting into fights when you're not wearing gloves?"

"First off, my dad doesn't call me names, except 'Slugger'. We have fun with real boxing gloves. He doesn't hit hard. He just keeps me from landing a blow to his body. You can tell he's enjoying himself because when I start jabbing at him really fast and hard he starts laughing."

"Sounds like fun for both of you."

"It is. He boxed Golden Gloves. Have you heard of that?"

"We had a jailer that boxed Golden Gloves but that was in his younger days before he joined the department."

"My dad boxed middle weight. Do you know how much he weighed?"

"I have no idea."

"He was 165 pounds. But he says he hasn't been at that weight for ten years. Do you know my dad?"

"We've met a couple times. I like him. I hope we'll be meeting again soon."

"What do you mean? Because of me?"

"Yeah, I'd like to visit with your parents and Mr. Allison. Has he been in to talk to the principal about this?"

"No, not yet."

"Is he planning on it? How about your mother?"

"My mother spoke with Mr. Allison yesterday but just for a few minutes. My dad's talked to Mr. Allison before, but he's not satisfied with the way he runs the school."

"I'll have to talk to Mr. Allison and see what he wants to do. This is his school, but he's told me that he appreciates me working with classes on conflict resolution. He might not want me talking to parents. I still think I can help, but I'm not saying I can keep people from picking on you. Sometimes things are unfair. You know that."

"I know."

"I've really enjoyed talking with you. You've

told me that you're tired of people making fun of you, that the harassment is coming especially from Terri and her friends, and that they do it a lot when teachers aren't around. What about the rest of the students?"

"I get along fine with about everyone else in class, but we're not exactly close friends or anything. Terri doesn't say stuff to me when she's by herself, but when she's with Amanda and Tiffany she gets mean and sarcastic."

"And tell me what she said to you. Wasn't she making fun of your skin color?"

"Yeah. She said that I couldn't go outside for recess because I'd be invisible if I took my clothes off."

"And she didn't hit you, right?"

"No, but she was in my face."

"Okay. I was just checking on what I'd heard so I could picture how it happened."

"As usual, she was showing off in front of her friends."

"It may sound like I'm taking Terri's side, but I'm not. She has no right to be making fun of you. School is supposed to be a safe place for everyone both emotionally and physically. There just has to be another way of getting Terri to stop what she's doing. And you still have no regrets for hitting her?"

"I could lie. It would probably be easier to just say I'm sorry for what I did. Is that what you want?"

"No! I'm just reviewing what you've told me. I think it's best to be clear on what's going on. If I were being made fun of all the time I don't know what I'd do. It would be difficult to go to school."

"It is. My mom and dad are even thinking about having me finish the year at another school or home school me."

"Oh, really?"

"Yes, only mom is gone so much with her job. But she says a lot of her work is done sitting at her computer on the Internet, so she could do that at the house. Dad's home, either in the shop or outside the rest of the time, fixing cars or training horses. I could help him."

"Home schooling is not just about repairing cars or riding horses. Preparing lessons is a lot of work. It's a good fit for some families, but it needs to be researched ahead of time. I just hope this school can become a safer place for you. What do you think?"

"I'd rather be with my friends here than by myself at home. Actually, I'm rarely by myself at home. When my parents are busy I take care of my little brother, Bud, and my sister, Catalpa. But I'd like to see my friends more. Holly has a favorite Appaloosa she rides when she comes over."

"Suanna, this conversation seems to be filled with a little bit of everything! I've certainly enjoyed our talk. Not everyone would open up like you do. I appreciate that about you. Now, I know you have work to do. I hope I'll be seeing you back in class next week."

"Goodbye. Thanks for stopping in to see me. Say hello to Holly for me."

"Okay. Oh yeah, next time we talk will you

tell me if there is some sort of guideline or creed about when or when not to use your boxing skills on others?"

"You can protect yourself."

"Okay. I'll talk to you about that next time."

"Bye."

19

BEING DIFFERENT

"ARE YOU IN TROUBLE?"

"Have you ever felt left out and not good enough? I really wish my friends would accept me for who I am and not leave me out."
—anonymous note in classroom question box

"**A**re you staying for our Christmas party?" I was asked by the fourth-grade student.

"Yes, Officer Potter, would you like to stay for treats?" Mrs. Fauley echoed.

It was only then that I noticed the pink cupcakes. Suddenly I could taste sugar in the air. I was thinking about sticking around for the party when I saw Matthew, one of the students, leaving the classroom without asking permission. He was carrying a book.

"Where's Matthew going?" I asked.

"He's a Jehovah's Witness so he's sent to the office to be away from the celebration," I was told.

I made a snap decision. I quickly hurried out of the room and caught up with the slow moving youth. As we walked down the hallway I asked him what he was doing and he replied: "Going to the office to read."

"Are you in trouble?" I probed.

"No, our family doesn't celebrate Christmas, so I have to leave the room until the party's over."

Maybe I was over-identifying but I felt there was nothing more important for me to do than to be with this child at this moment. Matthew took his place in the hallway on a chair that I had always thought was reserved for kids in trouble. That seemed wrong under these circumstances. In reality the chair served many purposes. It was an oasis for parents shuttling children, a comfort station for students ill or injured, a taxi-cab stand for students waiting for their unpaid chauffeur to arrive and to then be hurried off to distant appointments. And now I realized it could also provide a quiet place for a child to read.

Since he wasn't in trouble I wanted to join him, to somehow water down this moment of self segregation from his classmates, despite the fact that he had had years to grow accustomed to this routine act. I felt that spending some time with him was the right thing to do and in the process I could learn how he handled this religious custom.

"What are you reading?" I inquired, noting that he already had the library book open to an early chapter.

"*Mr. Popper's Penguins*," he answered.

I asked Matthew if he would feel okay with me sitting down by him and sharing the book. "We could take turns reading to one another, a page at a time," I suggested.

He liked the idea and as I listened to his reading I gave him a genuine compliment on being a great reader. His reading level was well above fourth grade. Lots of practice. During all the birthdays and holidays that were celebrated in grade school, I imagined, there sat Matthew... reading, reading, reading.

We read for quite awhile. The story was entertaining. But, I was also reading between the lines about a child who was able to handle the rigorous treatment of isolation for being different. On one hand he was used to it, on the other hand he told me that he "sometimes missed the students having fun in the room."

I enjoyed my time with Matthew away from the festivities. It was the best party I ever missed.

* * *

When I visited Matthew's fifth-grade classroom the next school year I saw how he was still standing out by sitting down. On that particular day, after the lunch count, it was time for everyone to stand and recite the pledge of allegiance to the flag, except for one. Matthew was the elephant in the room that no one acknowledged. Instead of focusing on the stars and stripes I caught myself peeking at him sitting at his desk. Matthew's eyes were unfocused and his face expressionless as the rest of the class proclaimed their loyalty to the flag and country.

Later that day in the lunchroom I sat at a table of boys, one of which was Matthew, my *Mr. Popper's Penguins* reader friend. Over lunch the students' level of excitement increased as they reminded me it was Valentine's Day. They each had their opinion about the best time of day to have a classroom party. A majority of the boys liked the idea of having it in the afternoon. To Matthew it didn't matter. He told me, "My mother's picking me up at one o'clock. I get to go home before they start the party."

I also learned how the fifth grade teacher had a different classroom approach to some holidays. This public school educator chose to have a "fall festival" rather than Halloween and a "winter party" instead of celebrating Christmas. *"What an inclusive way of keeping the class together!"* I marveled to myself. I was well aware though, that this caring Christian woman was risking being targeted for having questionable values in the ongoing, fevered, culture wars. I wondered, *"Would she be in trouble for being different?"*

Under the new system of celebration Matthew said he wasn't going to the office to read as often as the previous year, and his mother wasn't picking him up as frequently. But despite the accommodating teacher, it seemed to me, that for many people there's always going to be the natural curiosity of what it's like when others celebrate their own religious or cultural holiday.

Matthew and I had this in common. When I grew up in Skokie, Illinois, a predominately Jewish community where the menorahs far outnumbered the homes with Christmas lights, I had day-dreamed about Hanukah. I experienced a different kind of exclusion. On Jewish holidays I was one of a few Gentile kids expected to attend class while the rest of the school had the day off.

Matthew continued to contemplate events outside his experience while growing up in Reno County. When he remarked to me, "I've never celebrated Christmas. Wonder what it's like?" I wondered where his curiosity would lead him. With all his experiences growing up I expected him to remain strong to his religious beliefs. But, I also knew there was a possibility that he would eventually embrace the very things from which he had so carefully been sheltered.

20

ABSTRACT TO CONCRETE

"HAVE ANY OF YOU EVER CALLED 911 BEFORE?"

"911. What is your emergency?"

The police radio on my duty belt attracts attention. Kids may correctly identify it as a walkie-talkie and I'll ask them why they think it has that name. Sometimes I'll leave it turned on so that we can try to interpret the broadcast conversations. If the students are about third grade or older we might briefly discuss ten-codes or abbreviated talking.

I'll tell them about the dispatchers who work answering the emergency 911 calls. These are the same people who talk with us on our police radios—the main one in the patrol car and the smaller, mobile one we carry on our belt. In recent years dispatchers are more likely to send patrol officers messages to read on the vehicle's mobile data terminal (MDT). It offers greater privacy and accuracy without clogging the airwaves with chatter.

The students and I discuss what the word emergency means and under what circumstances someone, especially a child, might call the emergency number. I ask the students if anyone has ever called 911 because of an urgent situation. Some admit to having called the number when they were pretending. Of course, I'll caution them to not play on the telephone and to only call 911 when it's really necessary. Then I'll ask them, "What are the telephone rules in your house?" After a discussion, I'll conclude by telling them to talk to their parents or caregivers to continue the conversation.

* * *

One primary grade school teacher gave me some feedback on my classroom 911 training a few days after visiting her class. A boy's mother had warned him to never use the microwave oven when she wasn't home. He did so anyway. In her absence a potato exploded in the oven. "He knew he would get killed" when she returned home, so he called 911. The dispatcher explained to him that his situation was not the type of emergency they could do anything about.

* * *

During class tours at our law enforcement center children are most interested in seeing the jail but the emergency dispatch center is another favorite. The supervisory dispatcher usually cautions the visitors to only use 911 in a real emergency. Sometimes we'll even hear the often told story of a father who was explaining to his young son how to make an emergency telephone call. He picked up their home phone, dialed the three digits correctly, but hung up before the first ring. Seconds later the father answered the telephone, surprised to discover it was the city-county dispatch center. "Is there an emergency at this location?" the voice asked. He hesitated a second and was then questioned if there were children playing on the phone. Reluctantly, sheepishly, he admitted he was the one "playing" on the phone but for instructional purposes only. Both father and son got a lesson that day.

The dad hadn't realized that the telephone connection was completed prior to the actual ring on his end of the line. Since this occurred during an earlier technological era, he was also astonished to learn that the newly installed, enhanced 911 system, immediately displayed his address and phone number on the computer screen, thus allowing for the return caller to probe the circumstances.

Today the system continues to work superbly for identifying locations of real emergencies, even when a person, especially a child, doesn't know their own address. It also prevents most emergency prank calls from recurring. Once a child or youth, the most likely prankster, has the call returned by a dispatcher asking "What is your emergency?" and a uniformed officer makes contact at the residence, the problem ceases. Cell phones are another story, with many departments still unable to quickly locate a caller in need until more expensive systems are purchased with global positioning capacity.

* * *

I recall a first grade class I visited where the topic was personal safety. After my presentation, I received a number of stories. One personal narrative was shared by a girl who told the class about calling 911 because of a family crisis.

She was in the house with her mother and grandfather. He "was real drunk." He hit her mom in the stomach so the girl dialed the emergency number. Just when the dispatcher answered, the girl's grandfather knocked the phone out of the six-year-old's hand. A minute later the telephone rang, the girl answered it, and it was the dispatcher calling back to see if there was an emergency. Instead of playing with a toy telephone, the child was intervening between two adults, who one would hope would be her positive role models. The storyteller ended her brief account by further explaining that her grandfather was in jail for a week.

I found out afterwards from the classroom teacher that the girl lived with her father but had been visiting her mother for the weekend. After the reported domestic violence, visitations between the girl and her mother or grandfather were required to be supervised.

Immediately upon ending her story I held this young and experienced girl up as a model citizen. She was sitting down, but I was looking up to her with admiration.

My concluding remarks praised her: "Even though I'm much older than you, you are my hero for today! You were willing to get involved, to help out in an emergency. You did the right thing in a difficult situation."

Then, addressing the class I said: "Let's all give her a round of applause for knowing what to do and then doing it."

* * *

On a day off from school a fourteen-year-old girl was alone inside her rural home while her parents were away at work. The girl heard knocking at the door and became suspicious. Scared, but courageous, she called dispatch and gave them all the vital information officers needed to locate the house in the country.

The would-be burglars wanted their car off the road and easily available to load up with stolen property so they parked it up by the house. It just so happened that the vehicle was directly outside the window from where the teen was calling, so she was able to give an accurate account of the license plate.

The emergency telephone call was interrupted not long after it started when one of the burglars who had entered the home heard the frantic girl's voice in the other room. After he picked up an extension phone he realized in a flash that he was listening to a recognizable description of his crime—aggravated burglary—in progress. The criminals quickly ran from the residence without a face-to-face encounter with the teen. But as they hurriedly left, entering the getaway car, the scared but observant girl continued to contribute further detailed descriptions, including the color of the intruders' shoelaces. As the offenders' vehicle accelerated out of the long driveway, the young teen told the dispatcher which direction the car was going. Waiting for responding officers to arrive at her house she was able to shock the dispatcher when she spotted the criminal's vehicle return to the area in a confused attempt to get back to town. Before long they picked up a police escort, were stopped and had their identities confirmed down to the color of the laces of their shoes.

Sometimes our youth can really teach us adults a lesson or two about responding to urgent circumstances. The question still remains today, "Who was more surprised that day, the young teenager or the burglars?" There was pure drama in every word on that 911 call from the first two exclamatory sentences of "Please help me! There are two guys and they're trying to get in!"

* * *

I often wonder what happens to the children I've talked with in school. I've met many of them years later in jobs ranging from tow truck drivers, school teachers and attorneys. A couple of others have startled me with, "Hello, Officer Potter," from inside one of our county jail cells.

Did the six-year-old girl, an adult now, who called 911 to help protect her mother, ever consider being a counselor at a sexual-assault center? Or is she trapped in a relationship with an abusive partner? Does the former fourteen-year-old girl who was responsible for catching the bungling burglars, sell home security systems or is she employed as an emergency dispatcher, maybe even a police officer? And if she's a parent now, what does she tell her children when, inevitably, they are left alone at home? While she knows from firsthand experience that calling 911 works, how can she ever tell her children to not answer a knock at the door? Just how much do a handful of experiences in childhood influence our future?

21

PRIVATE PARTS

"WILL SUSIE BE SAFE AT HOME?"

"Remember the three personal safety rules. Say no! Get away. Tell someone. And if the first person you tell doesn't believe you then find someone else to tell until you're believed." [23]

I remember waiting in the hallway by the office for the first grade class to enter the lunchroom. Here they come! As the boys and girls pass me they hold out a hand for me to touch while many also ask for me to sit by them at their table. Then the girl I need to talk to walks by and asks for me to sit between her and the boy at the end of the line. *"Perfect!"* I think.

"Yes, I will. Thank you for asking," I reply.

I eat lunch with kids at different schools all the time without asking them private questions, but today will be different. I suspect that Susie has been sexually abused. I need to find out if she can go home after school to a house where she will not be a victim, a target of abuse. I need to know if this little girl, maybe seven-years old, is safe from being molested. Her answers to a couple of questions will determine my schedule for the rest of the day and possibly into my evening.

It's amazing to me that just a few answers to certain inquiries can alter our day and definitely affect the world and life of a child. And while these are personal questions, adults can never ask them enough. There is one theme...do you feel safe?

I pick up my silverware, then a napkin, skip the milk and grab a tray. The cooks recognize me and I win a sizeable portion of vegetables before meeting Susie for a walk to the first grade table. As we join the other students I marvel at the excitement of the lunch hour. Eating, being with friends, and being able to talk freely is definitely fun. I remember the two-cent cartons of milk from my grade school days and I wonder what they cost today.

At the table, first graders are discussing the food on their plates. They struggle to open the same half pint milk cartons with the same flavors, white or chocolate, that I struggled with as a child. The boy I was supposed to sit next to is beside me all right, only he's standing as he eats. Who knows, he may be in early training for a job as a cook or a chef. I'm asked several questions about my meal without milk. Children want to know if I forgot it, if I like it, and if I'm allergic to it. I explain I don't drink it anymore but that when I was their age I loved cold milk.

I catch Susie looking at my gun, safely in its secure holster.

"Don't touch it. It's not a toy," I warn.

Then, out of nowhere she asks me: "Do you know my brother?"

I know three of her brothers so I ask, "Which one?"

"Levi."

"Yes, I know him but I haven't seen him for a few years. Does he live with you now?"

"Sometimes."

"Who else do you live with?"

"My mom and dad."

"Tell me about Levi."

"He's cool!"

"What makes him cool?"

"He wears sunglasses that are too big for him!"

"Is he nice to you?"

"Yes, most of the time."

"What about when he's not nice to you?"

Then she shields the right side of her mouth with her right hand and leans toward me to whisper. I get smaller, bend my head, right ear towards her. I'm staring at the table, but I'm listening with full concentration. What will she reveal? Her secret?

"I don't like it when he flips me off."

I'm thinking she means he raises his middle finger to her as a rude gesture but for some reason I don't ask for a clarification. Instead I ask, "What do you do when he does that? Do you tell anyone?"

"I tell my parents."

"What do they do?"

"They tell me to go to my room and play."

Just before the lunch hour I had a class with the first grade about their personal safety so my next question is not as out of context as it at first sounds. During the classroom visit I showed a video and talked with the children about good reasons and bad reasons for taking off their clothes. I even told them that boy's "private parts" are covered by a one-piece bathing suit and girl's "private parts" are covered by a two-piece bathing suit. It was then that I couldn't help but notice Susie's immediate physical reaction.

Already a small girl, before I had completed my sentence she had visibly shrunk. In a fluid motion she wilted or regressed to a sitting fetal position. As she leaned forward her legs came together, locking knee to knee with each hand arriving quickly to be clamped protectively over her lap. Then she looked around the room for others to mirror her feelings. As her bright blue eyes searched for someone, she found no one that was willing to reflect her level of discomfort. But I had seen enough. In one moment she had told me of a world of experience that was hopefully well beyond the grasp of most seven-year olds. I knew I had a job to do before school was out. My ultimate question was, *"Would Susie be safe going home after school?"*

So, in this context of having just talked to the class about good touching and bad touching, I asked Susie: "Has your brother, Levi, ever touched you in your private parts?"

"Yes," she replied.

"Where are you when your brother touches you?" I continued.

"At home."

"Where are your parents?"

"Outside."

"Do you tell anyone?"

"I tell my parents."

"What do they do?"

"They tell me to go to my room and play."

"When your brother touches you does he have his clothes on or off?"

"On."

I'm about ready to end my informal inquiry. I've got enough information to have others follow up much more thoroughly with a professional line of questions, beginning with establishing if this girl knows the difference between telling the truth and telling a lie. She'll have to tell us what she means when she says "he flips me off." We'll all have to be clear about her understanding of the general term "private parts." Investigators may ask Susie to show them, with anatomically correct dolls, how Levi touches her when he's not nice.

"Does anyone else touch you in your private parts?" I continue.

"No," she replies.

I'm amazed at how easy it is to have a personal conversation about inappropriate touching over lunch at a table with twenty children. The beauty of the brief interview is that it takes place in a comfortable, non-threatening setting for Susie. She has her friends all around her and yet there is also privacy due to the increased volume of children's conversations. The social setting, especially with food present, helps create an atmosphere advantageous to a student sharing private stories, stories that for now at least, I have every reason to believe are true encounters.

Between my first grade class presentation when Susie waved what I considered a red flag about her personal safety, and our lunch interview, I have talked with the principal. She agrees that Susie has demonstrated other behaviors that haven't proven anything wrong but in their totality certainly point towards the need for further inquiry.

The principal and I communicate about my early findings and we agree that I will begin the official report to further investigate if Susie has been abused. We are well aware that the law describes us as mandatory reporters in the case of suspected child abuse. We also know that the criminal justice system can work very slowly. What I still have difficulty in accepting— and I'm an insider—is how long it takes for Social Rehabilitation Services (SRS) and law enforcement to formally investigate the possible abuse. I know it's about limited resources and heavy case loads. But I also think about how every day's delay puts the youngster and the investigation at risk. Once word of the child's concerns are known by a possible suspect— especially if it's a family member—then parental intimidation of the child may cause the young person to never again take the personal risk of seeking help by telling the secret truth.

Susie represents every vulnerable child that is a potential target or victim. No person, especially a child, warrants such treatment. But I know that the sooner abuse is discovered and stopped, the sooner there's an opportunity to start the healing. Families that live lies that are destructively deceitful soon have a myriad of other problems connected to their web of distrust. Some children act out by lying, stealing, hitting and bullying, physically hurting themselves or displaying promiscuous behavior. In contrast, other targets—victims, or survivors—may hide passively inside their battered vessels with feelings of self-deprecation. They try to just get by or work terribly hard at being the perfect child obsessed with pleasing others while searching for healing praise.

If Susie has been hurt physically then surely she's suffered emotional damage. I tell myself that she can triumph over any abuse. I've seen it happen before. Susie, like others I've known, is young and alert. I believe she can overcome this hardship. I want her future to be unlimited. With help she can use her life experience to help herself and others. Will she grow up to be a teacher, counselor or movie star? Who knows? But right now, most importantly, she needs the opportunity to be a child in a safe and healthy environment, one that is nurturing and has structure.

Before I leave the school, I learn that her brother, Levi, is out-of-state for the foreseeable future. So he won't be a threat to her...for now. My thoughts are interrupted when I see her walking towards me down the hall. As if to assure me that all is well she says: "You're the nicest policeman I know."

I smile and laugh. "I'm the only police officer you know!"

"I know other police officers from TV, but you're the only real one I know."

As I enter my patrol car for the drive back to the station I wish the best for Susie. Unbeknownst to her there will be interviews in her near future when others will make major decisions affecting her young life and the life of her brother. I haven't proven Levi is guilty of anything and

I'm also aware that when Susie's parents get involved in the interview process they could be her best ally or her worst enemy. Anything can happen, especially when one family member accuses another of inappropriate touching.

* * *

When children are repeatedly victimized I wonder what the experience does to them personally, socially and spiritually. At what point do they stop trusting family, adults in authority, whatever spiritual connection they may have once had, and most importantly, when do they stop trusting themselves?

I live for the day when all children, our greatest resource, are treated with the respect they deserve. Our young ones shouldn't have to worry about whether or not to tell a parent, guardian or teacher about the circumstances of being an emotional or physical target of abuse. And when they muster the courage to tell, I hope that the caregiver will be able to listen, comprehend and then to be supportive and loving. All children are entitled to have their family, their school and their larger community help protect them. It's only right. When a child does tell of being victimized he or she should receive real assistance, help far beyond the parental advice of "Go to your room and play."

22

JUDGING OTHERS

"YOU HATE *EVERYBODY* IN THE STATE OF GEORGIA?"

"You can't shake hands with a clenched fist."
—Indira Gandhi [24]

On the second day of Social Problems and Solutions class we divide the youth into groups of three or four students each. Then each group is given a handout sheet asking the participants to discuss questions about commonalities and differences. Once they've come to a consensus they will write down their answers, knowing they will be asked to report back to the entire class.

Under "things we all like" common answers are sports, food (pizza), chocolate, sleeping, animals, hanging out, shopping, listening to music, talking on the phone and watching movies.

Under "things we all dislike" homework is usually on the list. Other items include being grounded, school, school lunch, certain foods (Brussels sprouts), pimples, specific school subjects or classes, siblings and drugs.

Prior to each small cluster of students discussing "how we are all different" they're challenged to go beyond the obvious of physical characteristics, to dig deeper. This results in a wide range of answers including their place of birth, pets they own, sports and hobbies they enjoy, and to things they may be proud of like, "my bowling average" or "I'm in a community play."

On this particular day a seventh-grade boy, Jeff, is reporting for his group. He has just told everyone he dislikes Georgia.

I have a question for him. "You listed Georgia as a dislike. Do you mean a person by the name of Georgia or the state of Georgia?" I inquire, genuinely curious.

Jeff speaks up, "The state, I hate everybody in Georgia."

"You hate everybody in the state of Georgia?"

"Yep."

"Have you met everyone in Georgia?"

"No."

"In a couple of weeks my wife and I are going to visit my father-in-law and his family in Georgia. Have you met them? Do you hate them?"

"No, I haven't met everyone. I haven't met them. But I hate everybody I've met in Georgia."

"Oh."

Another group, this one with four students, reports on their list of likes, including that they all like the color blue. Their group reporter comments that they are all wearing blue which a student misunderstands as meaning the entire class, not the reporting group, as wearing blue.

"I'm not wearing blue," states Jeff, ready for a challenge, obviously thriving on the attention.

I'm ready. "Is your tee-shirt dark blue or black?"

"Black," he confirms.

Before I know it he is telling me I'm wearing too much blue! This is simply great conversation for a new group of students on our second day of school. I can see that Jeff will be the class provocateur, willing to speak up and give contrast to our theme of social problems and solutions.

"I'm wearing too much blue?" I ask, amazed at the conversation.

"Yes."

"You're telling me that the clothes I'm wearing are too blue? First you tell us you hate everyone in Georgia. Then you tell me I'm not wearing the right amount of blue! You're looking for some real trouble going around telling people you hate them when you don't know them, then telling people their clothes are the wrong color!"

"It's too much blue."

This is wonderful. We've known each other for one class and we're playing. I'm smiling in wonderment, getting louder, and everyone is laughing. Jeff is a seventh-grader who hasn't had a growth spurt yet so our sizes contrast. Is he too short? Am I too tall? I don't go there. Funniest of all, the blue he's criticizing is my deputy uniform! The class is about to end but I get up and put out my open hand to Jeff as I tell him, "I like you. Since the class time is about up let me promise you that we will revisit this subject very soon."

He extends a hand as he asks, "Does this mean I get something from you, like a treat?"

"No, it means that I like you. Nothing else. No food."

"Oh."

As the buzzer rings, the class exits and I begin to imagine the lesson we'll have on stereotyping, bias, and prejudice. Maybe that should be the next lesson, I think. Also, I'll ask Jeff privately, if it's not too personal, why he hates the people he's met from Georgia. It might be appropriate for a classroom discussion or it might not.

Jeff has clearly had an effect on me. After he has publicly proclaimed he hates everyone in Georgia it gives me an idea. When we visit Cartersville, Georgia in a couple of weeks I'll bring back a bumper sticker for him that proclaims: "I LOVE GEORGIA."

* * *

We make our satisfying trip to the great state of Georgia, but I'm in disbelief because after looking in a dozen shops we can't find a single bumper sticker! I settle on a key chain in the shape of a peach that simply says: "GEORGIA." And by the time I get to Kansas I know what I'm going to say when I present this special gift to Jeff.

* * *

I call Jeff up to the front of our small class. "Jeff, I have a gift for you. First off I need to tell you that sometimes I can be mean. I was going to get you a bumper sticker that said, 'I LOVE

GEORGIA.' Since we all know you hate Georgia, I might have gotten a laugh from the class, but then you, in turn, would have probably crumpled up the sticker and thrown it in the trash can." Instead, I take out my gift, "I got you this key chain. I hope you hold onto it. And here's something to remember: Even though you may hate everyone in Georgia, I want you to know that not everyone in Georgia hates you."

23

Form Follows Thought

"WHAT DO YOU BELIEVE ABOUT YOURSELF?"

"If you think you can do a thing or think you can't do a thing, you're right." —Henry Ford[25]

After everyone was seated I instructed each student to take out a sheet of paper. This was immediately followed by groans I identified as emanating from two boys. Why was I surprised? Silly me. But it allowed me an immediate example for the introduction.

"I wonder what you're thinking when just taking out a sheet of paper makes you moan?"

"It means homework," Brad explained.

"It's the beginning of class. What does that have to do with homework?" I questioned, truly confused.

"If we don't get it done in class then it becomes homework."

"Oh."

Bobby explained his point of view. "It means we're going to have to do work." When he said that four letter word, w-o-r-k, I could have sworn it took on a disgusting, if not diabolical tone.

"Well, we *are* in school," was my only comment, thinking how different people are in their experiences and expectations.

Then I gave the assignment. "Write down a belief that you have about yourself." Subsequently, I watched the looks, the befuddlement, and the pencils lying in wait atop the desks with no indication that they'd ever be stroked again. Just what kind of assignment was this anyway?

That's when my classroom guardian angel of instruction, Michelle, asked her clarifying question: "Could you give us an example?"

It gave me the opportunity to back up, to review the concept of beliefs I had briefly introduced in the last class. I went to the chalkboard and drew a table. Since Annie had been absent, I told her that I'd review what we had previously talked about. But while I was explaining it to her, the class of thirteen was involved with one common reason to listen and understand. They'd been given an assignment to do now, not for homework. And, it had to be written down, with it still momentarily unclear whether this was to be shared, collected or graded. I had caught them off guard. Their blank papers were reflecting the brightness of the overhead ceiling lights, in contrast to the slowly pulsating level of classroom creativity, a dim glow in the blank stares of fertile minds.

But the soft glow, mimicking the class discussion, began a gradual increase in activity and power. We were examining beliefs and our two examples centered around drugs: drugs are cool vs. drugs are harmful. I asked the class to think about how a person might explain their support for each statement. The table I had drawn, with its four legs, was representative of a belief.[26] I asked the class to come up with four references, or legs, to support the belief that drugs are cool.

"If you believed that drugs are cool what would support that conviction?" I got the impression the students were a bit surprised that I, a police officer, would be examining why people supported the use of drugs, but they began offering ideas.

"To fit in."

"To be cool."

"To feel good."

And finally, "To do their own thing."

"Good job!" I declared. You're really getting the idea. Now I don't want you going home and telling your parents or guardians that I was telling you reasons to use illegal drugs or legal drugs in an unhealthy way. Let's look at reasons people might give to support their belief that drugs are harmful. Who has an idea?" And the hands began shooting up like fireworks on the fourth of July.

"Poor health."

"Kills brain cells."

"Lose your memory."

As I wrote these supporting references on the board I was feeling the enthusiasm from our classroom community. It affected me, as I was smiling, happy to be on a roll of student participation.

"One more," I said, even as I could see more hands waving.

"Money."

"How much would a year's worth of cigarettes cost if they purchased one pack every day?" I asked.

After quickly agreeing on an average price and how many days were in a year, hands were up to announce the sizable amount of money, over a thousand dollars, spent on an unhealthy habit. I followed up, asking them what they'd prefer to buy for themselves, rather than tobacco, if they saved that amount of money. Clothing was a popular answer.

When I told the class that we had enough answers they democratically disagreed, keeping their hands up in anticipation of participation. I loved it.

"Jail."

"Lose friends."

I realized we were making real progress so I played with them. "We've got to stop. A minute ago you had nothing to say, now everyone wants to share. We've got to get back to Michelle's question that she asked at the beginning of the period."

"Car wrecks."

"Hurt family."

"Do damage to an unborn child."

This wasn't the time but I knew that a discussion on fetal alcohol syndrome would be a potential lesson when we followed up with our wider discussion on beliefs as they connected to social problems.

"Now that we've reviewed the idea of a belief being something more than an idea, that it has connections to someone's life, I'll get back to Michelle's question. You might have a belief

about yourself that is helpful or harmful to you."
I went over to the chalkboard and began writing
and slowly stated, "When I was your age I had
this belief: I AM STUPID."

There was a chorus of laughs. I felt a
flickering of fright, momentarily vulnerable,
then shook it off, and proceeded, knowing that
revealing a former disempowering fear would
cause the unpleasant experience to transform
into an empowering example.

"In the seventh grade I believed I was stupid
and I had my grades to prove it. I was a slow
learner. A *C* average was acceptable. Now, I
have two master's degrees. Those are advanced
degrees I earned after completing my first four
years of college. I went from believing I was
stupid to knowing that learning in school was
satisfying and fun. This happened because I
changed my belief system and found an area of
interest that sparked my passion. When you
change your belief system you change your
world. Then you can do anything."

Next, the students were given time to answer
the question of the day: "What is a belief you
have about yourself?" I also assured them that
they would not have to share their paper with
any other student, that it could remain private.

As the class was nearing completion I knew
that we hadn't gotten as far as I had intended.
I also knew that it was the best class I could
remember. To test that fact further I asked if
anyone had a belief that they were willing to
share in our final moments, before the bell rang.
The smallest person in class, an extroverted
boy named Kevin announced, "I believe that
even though people tell me I'm too small to be

competitive in sports that I will show them by being successful anyways."

"Exactly!" I shouted.

The bell rang. I began thanking everyone for their participation and willingness to take risks. Maybe my sharing a former belief of being stupid was the smartest thing I had done during class. The students reminded me that it's the teacher who is willing to be open and vulnerable who has the greatest opportunity to make a connection with students and at the same time to learn about himself.

24

SAYING NO

"DO YOU EVER GET PRESSURED AT WORK?"

[At the office]
"Would you like a piece of pie?"
"No, thanks, I'm on a diet."
"Oh, come on, it tastes good. It won't hurt you."
"No, really."
"Here you go. In case you change your mind."

———

During a sixth-grade class we were discussing ways of handling peer pressure. I was explaining how after a while, if you're consistent and congruent with your beliefs and actions, your peers will know you well enough to predict your behavior, at least about important decisions involving your character.

Then I told the class about a conversation I had with a co-worker that had just occurred the previous week while I was working security at a department store. While it wasn't anything major—I wasn't offered drugs or asked to beat someone up—it was an example worth sharing.

The employee wanted me to get her a snack out of a vending machine in the break room and then bring it to her in the men's department. She was clear about what she wanted. I thought I was equally as clear about my position.

I still remember how surprised I was that the sales associate wouldn't take "no" for an answer. But the fun part for me was getting a rare opportunity to say no over and over in different ways. It was almost like I was in a grade school D.A.R.E.® class where we were role playing, practicing "ways to be in charge."

"Will you get me some cheese curls?" she asked.

"I don't get food for people on the floor since it's against the rules. I want the boss to continue to trust me," I replied.

"Bill gets it for me!" she challenged, referring to another security officer.

"I'm not Bill," was my simple response.

"You won't get caught," she blindly promised.

"You're right about that," I concluded.

"I didn't get anything to eat before work!" she said in a victim's voice.

"Oh! That's different! Just get permission from management and I'll get it for you," I promised.

"I'd get it myself but I always get caught," she stated.

"I'll watch your area if you want to get something to eat," I offered.

"I don't have any place to hide it," she continued.

"I'll watch your area if you want to go to the break room," I repeated.

Then, finally, she made a decision and began

walking towards the break room saying, "I'll get it myself."

Amazed at how long it took her to understand the word "no", I said nothing.

I wondered, *"Hadn't she heard the word before?"*

25

GREED, ADDICTION AND ENFORCEMENT

"IF CIGARETTES ARE SO DANGEROUS THEN WHY ARE THEY LEGAL?"

[Seventh-grade student in hallway]
"Sgt. Potter, our sixth-grade D.A.R.E.® class finally paid off."
"What do you mean?" I asked.
"Saturday at the bowling alley a guy asked me if I wanted to smoke."
"What did you say?"
"No, thanks."
"That's great! What did he say?"
"Nothin'."
"Congratulations! You passed the final exam. I'm proud of you!"

———

S ooner or later in discussing the dangers of using drugs, including alcohol and tobacco, a student will raise his or her hand and ask the question. It's a question I still find daunting to answer: "If cigarettes are so dangerous then why are they legal?"

The question comes from our youth who

have been raised in an educational setting that teaches them to recite the pledge of allegiance about justice for all, to eat their nutritious school lunches and to not take any medicine at school unless it's dispensed by the school secretary or nurse. The young students can't figure out why a government that has the duty and obligation to promote the general welfare of its citizens, permits people (eighteen and over) to purchase and use a drug that's made from so many poisons and causes so much harm. It's a fair question.

Why would the government allow people to legally purchase a cigarette that contains over 200 known poisons, including carbon monoxide (car exhaust fumes), hydrogen cyanide (poison in gas chambers), formaldehyde (used to embalm dead bodies), and acetone (fingernail polish remover)?[27]

Why would the government allow cigarettes to be sold when they are responsible for 400,000 people dying prematurely every year in the United States?[28] That's greater than the entire population of Wichita, Kansas, and approaches the number of all residents in Kansas City, Missouri. Imagine all the inhabitants in either one of those cities gradually vanishing in a year's time until it resembled a ghost town.

The students are asked to take out their calculators and to figure out how many people on average die every day from smoking cigarettes: 400,000 divided by 365 equals more than 1,095 people—every day! In another attempt to grasp that abstract, mind-boggling annual figure we compare the number of deaths to two jumbo jets at capacity seating, crashing every day for a year with no survivors. In today's world if one jetliner crashes in a year there's international concern for the safety of the rest of the fleet and thorough investigations are immediately launched. It wouldn't take long for the entire airline industry to come to a halt if two commercial planes crashed in a day. So why, with cigarettes killing so many people, isn't something done to halt the slaughter of our citizens?

Is it because they, the smokers, ask for it? They know that the ride they're taking holds no promise of safety. They know that every time they purchase cigarettes they are forewarned of some looming health disaster: "Smoking causes lung cancer, heart disease, emphysema and may complicate pregnancy."[29]   Or is it because smokers don't die suddenly and unexpectedly as in a plane crash? Instead of succumbing in a giant fireball and making headline news, deaths from tobacco use are scattered over the country like a thousand staggered flickers from cigarette lighters at night.

Another related question is why a person, especially an adult, would use the drug, even though it's legal, around children. On one hand adults are telling kids to just say no to drugs, but with the other hand, tobacco stained fingers and all, they're smoking. When the parent exhales in the car or in the home, they're speaking volumes to their children as the maturing bodies become unwilling victims of the secondhand smoke.

The passive exposure increases the risk of ear infections which means children are more likely to require an operation to have ear tubes inserted to help drainage. Infants breathing cigarette smoke increase their risk of death from sudden infant death syndrome (SIDS) and weaker lungs. Secondhand smoke exposure causes lower respiratory infections (e.g., bronchitis and pneumonia) and for children who already have asthma it increases the frequency and severity of the attacks. School-aged children that have breathing problems, including coughing, wheezing, phlegm and breathlessness may have a cigarette smoking relative to thank since secondhand smoke exposure causes respiratory symptoms.[30]

No wonder our youth are confused about the dangers of drugs, especially the gateway drugs of tobacco and alcohol, and worse yet, about the decision making abilities of their own parents. However, my focus in class is never on the parents or caregivers. They're doing the best they can do. The students and I always talk about how the only person that is ultimately responsible for us is us, especially in making the choice whether to use harmful drugs.

I remember a Drug Abuse Resistance Education (D.A.R.E.®) culmination several years ago, where there was a fifth-grade girl named Diana who was so proud of her commitment to staying drug-free, that she was getting anxious when her mother didn't show up early to the school-wide ceremony. Finally, Mom arrived and the daughter ran over to greet her with a hug, then introduced me. Much to my shock the lady was wearing an attractive jacket advertising a well known brand of cigarettes! I was speechless. I recovered quickly enough to welcome her, to tell her how much I had enjoyed working with her daughter and despite being dumbfounded, I remembered my manners—I didn't lecture her on sending mixed messages to our impressionable youth.

Mom obviously cared enough about her eleven-year-old daughter to support Diana's enthusiasm in learning to resist negative pressures and to make good decisions. Nonetheless, every time I looked at Mom in the audience I thought of how ironic, how bizarre it was that she was at this celebration and wearing a colorful message encouraging smoking! But, I rationalized and realized that Mom was doing the best she could do. I could tell how important her approval was to her daughter and this parent wanted what other parents want: for her child to stay away from drugs, including cigarettes.

At the conclusion of the ceremony, as the younger classes were returning to their rooms and the fifth grade students were putting on their graduation tee-shirts with a drug-free message, I was approached by the Jacket Lady. Maybe I needed a lesson on being more accepting and less judgmental because she surprised me when she revealed to me an earlier conversation that she and her daughter had shared.

"Officer Potter," said the Jacket Lady, "I want to thank you for taking the time to teach my daughter to not do drugs. She's always coming home and telling me about the lesson she got in your class at school."

"I'm glad to hear that. I'm never sure if the kids talk much about school work once they leave the building," I replied.

She continued, "One day she came home and told me that the tobacco companies put nicotine in their cigarettes in order to keep their customers hooked. I told her that the nicotine was why it was so hard for me to quit smoking. Then I told her what I've always told her, that 'every single day I regret picking up my first cigarette. It's a nasty habit.' Thanks again, Officer Potter, for being someone she can look up to."

"Oh...Mrs. McArdle, you're welcome, but you're the one Diana really admires! She wants to be just like you."

* * *

When I'm back in the classroom, attempting to answer "the question" I often mention that the cigarette and chewing tobacco companies are greedy and manipulative. Since they sell a product that causes illness and death they must rely on the addictiveness of their product and problematic advertising in order to maintain a loyal customer base.[31]   Imagine needing a drug that is harmful, one that has the ability to trick the brain by programming it to believe the nicotine is helpful for one's everyday routine— from going to work to relaxing.[32] It's a seductive dance that appears pleasurable, but in reality the dancing partners are imposters. It's all a game of make believe as the cigarette companies (drug pushers) disguise their addictive product as pleasing while their dependent customers, needing a chemical to feel better, and unable to escape its deathly grip, continue the habit of paying for the very product that is endangering their health.

In our classrooms we talk about why people

start smoking and how hard it is to quit. Some start out of curiosity, some due to peer pressure, but often they begin because of a feeling that they aren't happy with their self-image. They want to be someone else. Many students have personal examples from their families of a relative who has tried to stop many times, sometimes successfully. I hear the pride and relief in children's voices when they tell me of a loved one who has quit. Others will share a sadder story of a family member whom they miss, who died of heart disease or cancer, a result of smoking or chewing tobacco. It's so difficult to explain how an average person can make such a destructive choice without the students fully understanding addiction.

"How many of you enjoy drinking pop or eating cookies?" I ask my attentive students. As proof that they are paying attention the hands shoot up. *"Have I triggered a sugar rush?"* I worry.

"Have you ever tried eating just one cookie when there were more available?" I continue. The question receives many nods and laughs as the students grin, talk to each other and admit that they seldom can eat just one. That's my point.

I'm ready to hear confessions, not testimonials about escaping junk food, as students describe their sugar addictions. You'd think we were at a Narcotics Anonymous meeting except that the sweets aren't against the law and the children haven't visibly seen many negative consequences yet from their eating behavior. But diabetes, as with most diseases, begins its destructiveness innocently enough.

I divulge to my class of students that I too have an occasional craving, not of sugar, but of salt. For me it can be satisfied with a small bag of potato chips from a vending machine during a fast-paced day at work. As with the young sweet tooths around me in the classroom, I'm able to satisfy the hunger without robbing a grocery store, pharmacy or bank. Unlike them, I minimize my use.

We talk about the power of advertising and media messages. I acknowledge to my class of students that I can understand why tobacco companies, always looking for additional profits, advertise the way they do. They spend billions of dollars every year to entice people to smoke.[33] In order to be successful, to receive a positive return on their investment, in their advertisements they show active and attractive people (often beautiful young actors with glistening teeth, inviting breath, flawless complexion and sexy voice) enjoying their product while having fun; not families coping with the inconvenience of a member forever attached to an oxygen bottle or families at a funeral grieving the loss of a loved one.

Students also want to know why law enforcement can't put a stop to illegal behavior. When we're talking about illegal drugs I make it clear from the start that the number one reason they flourish in our country and around the world is because of demand. Without the human need (psychological and physical) there would be no market for drugs. "Put a drug dealer or a cigarette company out of business—stay drug free," I proclaim. That's my simple answer although, in my opinion, all adults are obligated to do a much better job of helping raise healthy youth so that they don't require drugs to escape their personal problems. I know it's easier said than done.

Long ago governments started making financial deals with the tobacco companies. Instead of outlawing the manufacture, sale and use of tobacco our government decided to tax the harmful product.[34] Instead of halting its legal use, responsible today for billions of dollars in medical costs, the government chose to collect a portion of the profit to use for funding the budget.[35] It's so difficult to decline easy money. In the 1998 Master Settlement Agreement (between the top six tobacco companies and forty-six states—plus Washington, D.C.), "Big Tobacco" agreed to make annual payments to the states as reimbursements for health care costs related to tobacco use.[36] In other words, tobacco companies were permitted to continue to create illness if they promised to help pay for the health care for the sick people their product poisoned.

Because my students are so young I inform them of the monumental progress made in the last few decades on the nationwide perception of smoking. It's a sign of hope. Smoking in public places used to be considered by many a God-given right. Many of us can remember the days of airline travel when we suffered, breathing another person's cigarette smoke for two or three hours in a confined space. Or we recall entering a restaurant with great expectations of an enjoyable meal until we smelled the years of caked cigarette smoke resins on the walls, drapes, ceiling and furniture. Other times our right to enjoy a comfortable meal was stolen away by a single cigarette smoker enjoying programmed pleasure provided by a manufactured cancer causing device.

I tell my students about the physical discomfort I felt, when as a youngster and as a passenger in our family car, my dad would light up an occasional cigar. It made me feel sick, but my options were few to none. I would roll down the back seat window, hold my breath and try and devise a breathing filter using my shirt, but nothing could prevent the penetrating smell of smoke. I'd get a headache and feel nauseous. On those occasions, my sister or I would ultimately complain to Dad or to Mom, but we knew that in attempting to put out one fire we were lighting another. Dad had rights too! Even when he stopped lighting the cigar and it went out, the damage had been done to more than our lungs. We had paid an emotional toll for speaking up.

Some of the children respond that those conditions still exist in their daily environment. Their homes, where they reside for up to fifteen hours a weekday during the school year are similar to my stories of suffocating airline travel. They explain to me that where they eat, at their kitchen or dinning room table, there is the same ever present cigarette smell of smoke-filled reeking restaurants and a steady supply of irritating airborne chemicals. Sadly, as long as they are children living in the home of cigarette smokers, they have no opportunity to choose to live in a smoke-free atmosphere. They can't escape passive smoke unless their parents make a concerted effort to smoke outside, the adults choose to quit, or the child or grandchild, when older, moves to other living quarters. Hopefully, by the time the young adult relocates, he or she hasn't suffered any irreparable health problems, especially the potentially life-long addictive habit that they once abhorred—smoking or chewing.

Despite setbacks, times have changed for the better. In 1965 some 42% of adults in the United States smoked cigarettes.[37]   Today the percentage is closer to 22%.[38]   Many established smokers have quit while more children grow up choosing to be nicotine free.   This means there are less people dying of cigarette smoking and fewer children being exposed to the harmful effects of secondhand smoke.   It also shows great promise in breaking the cycle of addiction that parents have unintentionally passed on to their children.

It didn't happen over night. It took individuals, groups and laws to help transform the public attitude to a point where more customers and employees have guaranteed rights of being able to shop and work in a safer, more enjoyable environment. This was done with litigation and without making tobacco products totally illegal for adults.

The answer to many of our problems is education, not necessarily passing more laws. It's certainly true today. Prevention, intervention and treatment are important answers to our drug problems but hardly the best response to the global, corporate created catastrophe of addictive tobacco products. We can do so much more to reduce the number of smokers in the U.S. and abroad.

While 400,000 people die in the U.S. every year

from the number one preventable cause of death, most state governments invest a small percentage of the tobacco settlement money on prevention and cessation.[39]   Spending so little and allowing the tobacco industry to spend so much is absurd! It's comparable to the difference between a thirty second public service announcement on television at 3:00 a.m., versus a widespread tobacco industry marketing strategy of inundating the public with easy temptation and recognizable icons twenty-four hours a day. Social events at clubs, bars and college parties have been sponsored by the tobacco industry where they give out free cigarettes.[40]   Sporting events around the world, from race car driving to tennis and soccer allow the tobacco industry to reach large, young audiences, to get their image on television, and to project a picture of strength and vitality when the health effects of tobacco actually cause weakness and sluggishness.[41] Tobacco companies help promote customer loyalty and gain free advertising by offering their brand products to be purchased through cigarette coupon catalogs. These mail order or Internet items range from towels to tee-shirts and hats to jackets.[42]   But one place you're most likely to find cigarette marketing is in the privacy of your own home when you open the daily newspaper, a weekly magazine or use the Internet. While we've made progress, there's still no reasonable comparison between prevention efforts and aggressive marketing of tobacco.

As long as the tobacco companies continue to grossly outspend public health while prevention budgets are laughable, how can the rates of addiction decrease further? If our politicians don't have the resolve to make a dedicated effort for prevention and cessation strategies, when every day in the U.S. 1,500 kids become regular smokers, then this may be the time for advertising tobacco products to be restricted further.[43]   Efforts could be modeled after the World Health Organization's Framework Convention on Tobacco Control that works to reduce tobacco-related deaths and disease. One element in the treaty is to prevent tobacco companies from spreading their addiction to people around the globe by banning all tobacco advertising, promotion and sponsorship.[44]

Don't we owe it to ourselves and to the world to solve, not displace, our national problems? Shouldn't we lead other nations in helping restrict "Big Tobacco's" deathly grip?

26

Ripples in the Wake

"HOW MANY OF YOU KNOW SOMEONE WHO HAS ATTEMPTED SUICIDE?"

"He bit the bullet," I said.
"What do you mean?" he asked, confused.
"He shot himself. He's dead."
The man lowered his head and broke into tears. Sobbing, he informed me, "He was my friend."

———————

The middle school students have been advised that today we will have a visitor from the professional mental health community. Her topic? Suicide.

Mr. Lightfoot, the regular classroom teacher, has already shared his favorite quotation about the subject. "Suicide is a permanent solution to a temporary problem." He reminds us that sometimes a predicament that seems overwhelming one day will often lose its intensity by the next morning, after even a poor night's sleep.

I've told the class of students that the reason we discuss the subject is because the more accurate information they have about suicide, the more effective they can be if someday they are faced with a decision about how to help prevent someone from taking their own life. They need to know these things. They can make a difference. They can save someone's life. And the life they save may be their own. In our contemporary world of increased pressures, competition, and violence there's a much greater likelihood that a person's suicidal thoughts will surface. The students in this room, the earliest of teens, may have a peer confide a problem to them long before that friend seeks out an adult to tell, an adult who at times is too busy to listen and at other times unable or unwilling to take them seriously.

Then in walks our guest speaker and no matter how many titles I put before or after her name she prefers to be called Elizabeth. This approachable professional immediately connects with the students. She sets the tone for listening and sharing. I like how she instructs the youth to abandon their rows of school desks and to join her with their chairs in a circle. After introductions everyone is handed a piece of paper and instructed to anonymously write down a question about suicide for Elizabeth to answer.

Our visitor tells the group that when she was in seventh grade she didn't know of people who had attempted or committed suicide, but today it's not uncommon for youth to be more personally exposed to the rough realities of someone choosing death over life. To emphasize her point she asks the youth in the group to raise their hands if they know someone who has attempted this desperate act. About half the students acknowledge some connection, close and personal or distant and abstract. My hand goes up and I'm not bashful in admitting how the deliberate act has twice shocked my extended family and friends.

Later, when Elizabeth tells of the categories of people who attempt suicide the most often—teens and elderly, I have personal experience with both. Whether a fifteen-year-old cousin with the pain of heartache over a lost girlfriend and easy access to a gun, or an elderly aunt with a secret of deep financial debt, a decline in health and home delivery of medication, our family was stunned to its core.

Meanwhile, as the students think and write, Elizabeth begins presenting statistics on the lethal topic. The numbers are astonishing! In the United States over 30,000 people commit suicide every year.[45] We don't seem to notice that over a half million people every year require emergency room treatment as a result of attempted suicide in our country. And there are so many others that never get officially counted until they become more desperate, disturbed or depressed.

I'm glad to hear Elizabeth correct a major myth about suicide—that talking about it doesn't cause people to attempt it. She assures us that the hopeless act is preventable because there are usually warning signs. We are further advised that if someone is talking about suicide it's important to take that individual seriously, to remember that a problem that seems small to us may be monumental to them. What helps me understand this mystifying topic most is when Elizabeth assures us that most people thinking about suicide as an answer to their problems don't really want to die—they just want to stop feeling the overwhelming, excruciating pain of their problem.

She tells us that the warning signs of suicide go beyond someone making suicidal threats. A person may have experienced a significant loss like a teenager suffering the turmoil of breaking up with their first love, their parents divorcing or the death of a member of their family. An individual considering suicide may display erratic behavior, seem to have lost the ability to see anything good about themselves, be giving away treasured possessions or taking care of unfinished business before their secretly planned departure. They may be obtaining the means for taking their own life, displaying self-destructive or death defying behavior by taking unreasonable risks, or threatening to get even with someone for real or imagined injustices.

Elizabeth surveys the circle, observes the attentive teens holding or folding their anonymous questions, then directs the students to pass them to her. She unfolds them, reads each one, and makes positive noises, saying how good they are as she sorts them into categories. She is ready to answer a range of questions.

"What is the youngest age a person has killed themself?" she reads.

"There have been children as young as five and six that have committed suicide, but none so young in our community that I recall." As she says the age, our eyes open wider and our heads kick back as though there has been an explosion in our midst. A majority of us are shocked for the first time today. We wonder why they would do that. Elizabeth explains that these innocent ones may not even realize how real and deadly a gun is or comprehend that unlike television shows or the movies, when someone is killed they aren't acting, and they don't get a second chance to do the scene over.

Another question surfaces from the stack. "Who kills themselves more often, boys or girls?" Elizabeth reads. "What do you think?" she asks the circle of students.

"Boys," is the answer given by a chorus of participants, both genders voicing their opinion.

"Why do you think that, how come?" Elizabeth encourages.

While I'm thinking that boys are more reckless than girls, explanations materialize from the mouths of children.

"They don't share their feelings as often as girls," a feminine thirteen-year old responds.

"We get angrier than girls," a tall, lanky boy contributes.

"We know how to use guns," another boy states proudly, his ego intact.

"Yes," Elizabeth acknowledges. "Boys are more familiar than girls with guns and they have greater access to them."

She continues, "Girls attempt suicide much more often than boys, but they are more likely to survive. That's because when they take pills—unlike using a gun—there may be time to rethink the choice before unconsciousness or death. When someone takes an overdose or poison they usually don't go peacefully to sleep and die. Often the person becomes violently sick, they get scared and then they call for help. Sometimes, depending on the time factor, a person's stomach is pumped to remove its contents." It's not fun, but it's memorable.

"Whether someone attempts suicide with a gun or an overdose, if they survive, they may have life-long health problems due to a moment's despair. There have been people who have shot themselves in the face only to survive and to spend the rest of their life with a daily reminder of their desperate act. Brain damage is another potential consequence for survivors of self-inflicted gunshot wounds, people who choose pills or poison, and those that are interrupted when they are suffocating or being deprived of oxygen during the act of hanging themselves. There are adults who, years after their attempted suicide, are happily married with a family, but who are then forced to deal with the realities of their body organs failing, all because of a destructive decision made in their past. It just proves that every choice has a result."

Elizabeth takes a breath and reads the next question, "What is the most common way of someone killing themselves?"

She answers. "Like I said, the use of a firearm and an overdose of drugs are the most common, but some people hang themselves while still others commit suicide by driving recklessly in their car."

I reinforce the last comment. "When we work automobile wrecks, especially fatalities, we're not always sure if they're accidental or done on purpose. One of the first injury accidents I investigated was a car that drove head on into a tree. When I couldn't locate any brake marks on the road I questioned if this was a result of the driver falling asleep or due to an intentional act of the subject wanting to hurt himself. And when we work deaths that are apparently the result of a self-inflicted gunshot wound, unless there is a suicide note or witnesses, we may never be absolutely sure if it was an accident, suicide or even homicide."

Elizabeth reads on, "Do kids or adults kill themselves more often?" Then she asks, "What do you think?" A majority of the students voicing their opinion believe that adults commit suicide in greater numbers.

Elizabeth explains that adults do attempt and commit suicide more often than young people, but that for young people only accidents and homicides occur more frequently. Also, she informs us, the elderly have the highest rate of suicide, then asks us, "Why, do you suppose?"

The consensus of the students is that the elderly are more determined and ready to die because they may be terminally ill, have had a spouse die recently, or they may be under the belief that they are a burden to their family.

"When someone takes his or her life, especially an adult, they may think they aren't hurting anyone, but whenever a suicide occurs there are ripples in the wake. When a family member actively participates in this once unmentionable act, there is a greater likelihood that others in their family will consider it as an option when they are struggling with life's lessons. In killing themselves, an adult may inadvertently be contributing to the suicide of those they love most, the ones they may be trying to protect."

I can't keep quiet—it won't be the last time. "Like Elizabeth says, people who commit suicide may think it's a victimless crime, but their family members will have to deal with the circumstances for a lifetime. There are also the train engineers, truck drivers, emergency medical personnel and police officers that are pulled into the drama of life or death, sometimes put in the haunting position of being forced to watch or aid in someone's decision to die. I know that I've lost more than sleep thinking about bloody, stressful suicide scenes that have occurred during a shift working the road."

A student's hand shoots into the air so suddenly that I think she's going to need to run to the bathroom. Instead she must ask Elizabeth a question. "Has anyone ever committed suicide after they've contacted you, after you've talked with them?"

"Yes, but it's never happened right away," Elizabeth responds. "The couple of times when people have killed themselves it's been years later, well after the original emergency room consultation. But there's always that risk in this job. That's why we always want to err on the side of caution. Generally, we can talk with the person and tell them that as a precaution we'd like him to agree to be observed and tested so that we can give him our best treatment. If he won't agree, and we believe he is in danger to himself or others, we can get an order for him to be temporarily held at the psychiatric wing of the hospital. However, even with therapy and medication there are some people that are eventually going to kill themselves."

Thinking about the permanency of someone dying after being interviewed and released is mind boggling to me. Straightforwardly I comment, "I don't know if I could do your job. If I counseled someone and then they killed themselves I'm the one that would be depressed."

Before Elizabeth can respond, Tori, a bright thirteen-year old speaks her mind. Looking directly into my eyes she asks incredulously, "If you did your best why would you feel guilty?"

"Excellent! Tori, I like your thinking! You're right. I can learn from you." Again I visually add yet another young guide to the growing list of people I respect because of their thoughtful participation in my life. When they speak the truth it's so loud and clear.

We've had a lively class about a deadly topic. The final question, I think, is the hardest. "Are people who attempt suicide crazy?"

"Most of the people who attempt suicide are depressed, but I wouldn't call them crazy," responds Elizabeth. "When a person tries to kill himself that can seem pretty irrational to you or me, but to someone who is depressed it can be seen as a reasonable way out of their misery or pain. Actually, a critical time for someone who has previously attempted suicide and is still depressed, is when she starts to feel better. It sounds strange, but people who are severely depressed may have trouble just getting out of bed, let alone taking steps to kill themselves. Once a person starts getting their energy back they've been known to then carry out their suicidal plans. Depression is complicated and difficult to explain here, but it's a medical condition that affects twenty million Americans each year.

"There are suicides by people with mental disorders that you might call 'crazy' because of their unusual or bizarre behavior but these are a small number compared to the majority of people who appear 'normal' and seem to fit into our society. Other suicides are committed when people are drunk and obviously not thinking clearly. Under the influence, they often take risks they wouldn't normally take. Would you say a person is crazy if she is drinking and driving?

"I'd like to leave you with a few tips on what to do if you suspect a friend is considering suicide. Like I said at the beginning of class, if you hear anyone talking about hurting himself, take that person seriously. Be a good listener and don't judge them. No matter how good a friend they may be, don't get tricked into keeping a secret that could prevent them from getting professional help. If you have promised not to tell, that's a promise you must break. If your friend killed himself after you withheld vital information it would be a heavy and unfair load for you to carry. A friend who is thinking clearly wouldn't want you to have to live with that decision. By sharing with an adult your information or suspicion you can help save your friend's life. Hopefully, that companion will recover and be around to thank you for choosing to get involved."

The second hand on the clock is making a dash for the finish line and this isn't grade school where they remain in the same classroom most of the day. Soon these students will scatter to their other classes in the building. Elizabeth quickly passes out some suicide prevention material along with a toll-free emergency number that accepts calls twenty-four hours a day. I wonder how many of these young people will examine the written material later or save Elizabeth's contact information for future use.

I recall that a couple of weeks after one of our suicide prevention talks a student in our class informed a teacher of a new friend who was cutting herself and talking of suicide. The teacher told the school counselor and the counselor immediately had a private conversation with the student in crisis. When the specialized staff confronted the young girl with the facts, in a timely and caring manner, it made all the difference in this encounter. "Yes," she agreed, "I need help." When she told her newest friend about her thoughts of suicide it had been more than a need for attention. It was a cry for help. The girl's father was then contacted by the school counselor and he was able to get his daughter professional help. A life may have been saved because of a friend telling, not keeping, a secret.

* * *

When Kim, a friend of mine with mental illness, and I were discussing her disease, I told her how I thought schools were an appropriate place to discuss the topic. When she concurred I asked her to consider visiting our class in the future. I also shared the story of our professional classroom visitor who regularly speaks about suicide. I was encouraged by my friend's response because some people are surprised to learn that we talk to such a young audience about such a depressing topic. Kim said, "Middle school's not too soon. The first time I tried to kill myself I was eleven years old. I wish we had been able to openly discuss mental illness and suicide when I was a child. It might have helped me and others."

27

Parents Who Use

"WILL YOU TALK TO MY SON?"

"Do you know my dad? He's in jail." —I'm asked by children in the classroom, hallway and on the playground.

Some kids learn to be resilient and successful despite a parent or their home environment, but a family that appears dysfunctional has to cost the children something, at least heartache and mental anguish.

Like so many intricate stories, this one started with a telephone call.

"Sgt. Potter, I'm worried about my son. Do you have a minute?"

I learn that this single mother is anxious about her seven-year old, Joey. He's told her that sometimes on their visits his dad smokes marijuana when they're in the car together.

She is concerned and so am I.

I'm surprised when she tells me she didn't know whom to call until her older son, a former D.A.R.E.® student of mine recommended, "Call Sgt. Potter."

I learn how Joey is put into a seemingly impossible position. He has love for and loyalty to his father, yet he's been told not to tell his mother of this illegal activity. On top of this the father actually asks his son if it's okay for him to smoke! By my way of thinking, this is backwards, unhealthy and dysfunctional. When the adult asks the child if it's okay to smoke there is an unbelievably high degree of stress on the youngster. Joey replies to his dad, "Yes, it's okay," because he doesn't want to make his father angry. He says, "Yes," because his dad tells him he needs it because he's feeling sad. Dad is setting his son up for all kinds of potential problems. Will Joey use drugs or alcohol in order to feel better? Will he use a depressant to relax or a stimulant to have fun because he missed out on the promise of playfulness in his childhood?

What Joey may not know, according to his mother, is that she gave her ex-husband a choice between their family and drugs. She tells me he chose drugs.

Mom is also telling me that Joey looks up to me as a role model and she thinks he would benefit if I could speak with him.

"Would you have time?" she asks.

"Yes, I'll make time!" I'd like to give him a healthier perspective on the choice his father is making and to let the young one know that he's being put into an unfair position of feeling like he's responsible for controlling his dad's drug use.

Mother explains that she and her two children are getting ready to move out of state, that her ex-husband, who has joint custody of the children, lives out of our jurisdiction, and that her car is broken down and has been in the shop for a week. On top of this the school year is just beginning.

The first thing I want to get clear in my mind is what Joey's mother is asking of me or the department. She tells me where this alleged drug use is occurring and the activity sounds like it's out of our county. Her attorneys have advised her that for now she must continue to permit the father to see his son even though the chronic marijuana user is refusing to take periodic drug tests. I arrange for her to speak with our juvenile detective, whom she knows, about the recommended course of action as far as which jurisdiction to contact in order to file an official report.

I tell Mother that I'd be willing to speak with Joey to let him know that there are other ways of dealing with sadness besides using drugs. I also inform her that I will not be interviewing him as a potential witness. That would only add to his feelings of confusion, guilt or betrayal over not keeping a secret between father and son. She agrees to my visiting the seven-year old at school and I explain that she will need to call the school's principal for me to have access to him for the interview.

I arrive at the school the next day over the lunch hour in order to speak to Joey, but first I contact the secretary and the principal. Gail, the secretary advises me that Mother has called and given permission for a sit-down talk.

Joey and I visit in the lunchroom at our own table. Now, with my height of 6'4" I'm expecting to be a giant next to the elementary school children but Joey is *so* little, smaller than I remember! We each grab a chair that reminds me of miniature doll house furniture, then start talking. I'm amazed at his conversation level. He tells me that next week he, his mom and sister will be going to Nevada. I'm told it's far away, but they can get there in a couple of days if the car's engine doesn't overheat. "It's in the shop being repaired," I'm informed.

"I'll send you postcards when we get there," the big, little man offers.

"That would be nice," I say and get a business card out and hand it to him.

It turns out that I'm not telling Joey anything he doesn't already know. I say to him, "Adults shouldn't be asking their children if it's okay to do drugs."

He responds, "I know that."

"When people get sad there are healthy ways to feel better without smoking marijuana," I continue.

"I know that. I don't smoke marijuana," Little Big Man responds.

"Because your dad smokes marijuana doesn't mean that you should follow that example."

This little boy sounds like the adult he's been pressured to become. "I don't smoke marijuana. I know it's unhealthy. My dad says he needs it because he's sad. He cries all the time."

I make sure Joey knows there is a difference between loving his father and approving of the choices his father makes. Finally I say, "It isn't your job to get your dad to stop smoking marijuana. That's his choice, but you can continue to love him whether he smokes or not."

We stand up so I can walk him to his classroom. I don't shake hands. I don't hug him. I'm not sure how to treat him. Will he be here next week or disappear over the weekend, a passenger in a car that might or might not overheat on the road to Nevada? How much will his life change in new surroundings? How often will he see his father then? And how much of a childhood does he have left?

Joey and I enter his classroom. He goes to look at a book while I speak with his teacher. She wonders how long Joey and the family will be here this time. She informs me that over the last several years the children have moved in and out of the school district at the whim of the parents. She tells me that the teachers figured up the total tumultuous times at eight! Eight! I wonder of the academic and social cost to the children from such an unpredictable lifestyle. Then I remember that parents do the best jobs they can do.

The family structure and economic conditions may dictate that Joey's parents, for their group survival, require periods of absence from the community—including school. Also, while it's easy to criticize Joey's father for making poor choices, part of it seems due to his reliance on drugs as a coping mechanism. Getting high doesn't solve any of his long-term problems but it offers him temporary relief in his stressful, chaotic world.

Despite my middle class expectations, Joey is not locked into a world of doom. He might become a responsible, compassionate counselor some day or choose any job or career he wants. But first, he needs to survive his childhood.

28

Support Systems

"WHAT PROOF DO YOU HAVE?"

"It is a wise father that knows his own child."
—Shakespeare[46]

"Who's your role model?" I asked.
"My parents," he replied.

Eye witnesses to a crime or alleged crime are often unable to definitively recognize the perpetrator, but sometimes eye witnesses accuse the wrong person. That's a fact we have to deal with in law enforcement. Sadly, by the time the investigation is under way, rumors may already be tarnishing the reputation of a totally innocent person. But since we want to solve the crime, we have to question people, and in doing so, victims and witnesses are interviewed as the suspects are developed (or the witness and victim accounts are discredited).

Beyond the movies they watch on television, school resource officers may be the first exposure many younger children have to our criminal justice system, so we take pride in having our contacts be friendly, positive experiences. However, on extremely rare occasions our interactions with children are negative, even disastrous. It can occur when we are in charge of an after-school gathering such as a bicycle safety course, skating party, or field trip, and someone makes an allegation against another person of some wrongdoing. What do we do? We investigate. First, like any good parent, we do our best to make sure some offense has really occurred, discover how serious it is, and attempt to understand the different sides of the story from all those involved.

* * *

One day on a field trip an accusation was made about a student, but because of caring, trusting, assertive parents, and supportive friends, an ugly situation became bearable. In the process an innocent twelve-year-old learned a lesson he should never have had to experience: being treated like a criminal.

A girl told her school resource officer that a five dollar bill was missing from her jacket's zipper pocket.

"Are you sure it was in your jacket to start with?" he questioned.

"Yes, I'm positive," she said.

"Could you have left it at home?" he continued.

No, I had it for spending on snacks."

"When was the last time you knew the money was there?"

"At home."

"Could it have fallen out?"

"No, my zipper's been shut."

"Where was the jacket?"

"With me."

"Have you had it with you the entire time?"

"Yes, except when we were having lunch at the park. It was warm outside. I left my jacket on the bus."

After the officer perused the seats and floor of the bus he made an announcement about the missing money to the students, mentioning who had lost it. In response, two students contacted him and told him that they saw a boy they didn't know on that girl's bus, by himself, near her seat, during the stop at the park. And a description? He had dyed blue hair!

The officer had the boys locate the blue-haired boy and point him out.

"Which one? Are you sure? Thank you."

The boy, who identified himself as Calvin, was questioned by the officer. The reason Calvin had been on the school bus? He had returned to retrieve his sunglasses.

Without enough evidence the officer decided to deceive. He used an accusatory approach with this juvenile that should have been reserved for someone who was known to be involved in a crime, not someone so young, without a parent present. He accused the boy of taking the money from the girl's jacket, told him there were witnesses that saw him do it, and that, "You better admit it or you'll be in more trouble. We need that money back. There could even be a charge here if it's not taken care of."

Calvin, in shock, talked with his friends. "I didn't do anything, but that officer says I was seen stealing it. What do I do?" Calvin and his buddies decided to pool their money to the tune of five dollars and have someone else give it to the officer. They asked a classmate to take it to the interrogator and tell him, "I found it on the floor of the bus."

But once the officer had the money turned in it made him even more suspicious. His inquiry as to when the currency was discovered revealed an unsure child. It wasn't too long until the obliging courier disclosed that he was simply carrying out a request from some students to turn in the money they had "found." A heartbeat later the investigator watched as the do-gooder pointed out the conspirator. It was again the boy with the blue hair, Calvin. With this new evidence, figured the cunning crime fighter, it was time for a full confession.

He was a bit surprised when Calvin gave another perspective. The pre-teen explained how his friends helped donate the money to help him stay out of trouble. But the officer didn't believe this story, seeing it as a cover-up for the crime. The cop concluded that turning in the money was a sign of guilt instead of a sign of desperation from a falsely accused youth. But with the money "found" the officer was able to appease the "victim" with its prompt "return." Satisfied with the results, he congratulated himself on the drama ending happily.

But Calvin wasn't feeling as fortunate about his problem-solving experience with the police. In fact, he was really perplexed as to how it had all happened. One minute he was having fun and the next he was being grilled by a no longer friendly officer. How had this nightmare occurred, he wondered?

When Calvin's parents picked him up after the field trip they noticed a change in their boy. He was subdued. Something was wrong. Before long, at first reluctantly, their son recounted the stressful episode. His folks listened, and then came to his rescue. Most importantly, Calvin's parents believed their son. The elders spent the evening on the telephone and spoke with Calvin's friends who had been on the field trip. All agreed, Calvin hadn't done anything wrong and that being on the bus in the vicinity of a jacket didn't mean that he had stolen anything.

First thing the next morning Calvin's father drove down to the Sheriff's Department to get the official's side of the story. After inquiries with administrative personnel, including the sheriff, he was able to speak directly to the stunned officer.

"My wife and I want to get more information about what happened with Calvin yesterday on the field trip," the parent stated. "He came home acting down and told us his side of the story. We've checked with his friends. Kids at school think he's a criminal. I know my son. He's a good kid, not a thief. I can't imagine him taking anything, especially money. If my son's done wrong there will be consequences, but what proof do you have that Calvin committed this crime?"

The officer explained about the report of the missing money, about the witnesses that put Calvin near the jacket, but admitted that he had been too heavy handed under the circumstances, allowing his street instinct to get the best of him. Also, he confessed, he couldn't say that Calvin had stolen any money just because he had arranged for an acquaintance to turn in the five dollars. Within moments the officer had apologized for the unfriendly fiasco.

But dad wanted more. This number one supporter of his boy, this role model who demonstrated faith, love, and discipline, wanted the officer to correct the wrong. He expected an apology to Calvin in person.

"Done," the officer agreed.

Before this cop could make arrangements to speak with Calvin he received an informative phone call about the recent field trip. He spoke with the mother of the girl who had reported the cash stolen. Much to his astonishment he learned that the five dollar bill had been removed from the jacket pocket prior to her daughter's field trip, but without the sixth-grader's knowledge! How did the parent explain the missing money? "I borrowed it back to buy a pack of cigarettes I needed." Then she concluded the conversation with, "This has all been a misunderstanding and we hope no one was hurt by the mix up. Sorry."

With this breaking news the officer made arrangements with school personnel to meet with Calvin one-on-one. He did apologize. Then this recovering cop took a remarkable step forward, asking the twelve-year-old if he would allow him to make another apology, but this one in front of Calvin's class and teacher.

"I think I just want to forget about it," said Calvin.

"Whatever you want to do, I know you've been through a lot in the last twenty-four hours."

"I'm just glad the money was found," the boy replied.

"Me too," said the officer.

"It's over," Calvin confirmed.

"Yes," echoed the SRO.

"Now I can forget it...but...if you talked to the class...what would you say?" Calvin cautiously asked.

"Well, besides my public apology of being wrong and explaining how the money was never stolen, your class could have a really good discussion on the law, rights, and the way adults like me sometimes treat children when we think we know best."

"Hmm...sounds interesting. You know, I'd like to be in on that class discussion. I could give my point of view of how I felt."

"Your opinion needs to be told. I know I've got a lot to learn! Again, I'm sorry this ever happened. You've already taught me a great deal about the quality of your friends, your family, and especially about your character."

"My parents are the best!"

"I like the way your dad handled all of this. He has a lot of faith in you. And, he was able to get this worked out without blowing up or making a federal case out of it. Amazing."

"He's always been there for me. Some of my friends wouldn't have had this support. What would have happened to them without an adult willing to be involved?" Calvin inquired.

"Good question, Calvin. For one, I think it would be a long time before they trusted a police officer, if ever again. Also, without an adult to show support by listening and taking action, a lot of people could have mislabeled them young criminals. How do you think you would have handled all of this without your parents getting involved?"

"Hmm...it was bothering me. I guess I would have just counted on my friends to keep believing in me. I don't think I would have done anything else except try and forget about it. I know one thing for sure—I would have *never called the sheriff!*"

29

IMAGINING THE UNIMAGINABLE

"IS OUR SCHOOL SAFE?"

"Could Columbine happen here?" *a teacher asked.*
"Yes," I replied.

While visiting a second grade classroom, preparing to speak on the topic of bicycle safety I decided to take a risk and open it up for questions from the students. Sure enough, the first few weren't about bicycle safety. In fact, the first one wasn't even a question.

"Officer Potter, we got a thirty day notice in the mail," said a girl with an engaging smile minus two front teeth.

"Do you know what a thirty day notice is?" I asked.

"It's when you need to find another place to live before thirty days are up," she informed me and her class of seven-year-old peers.

"I sure hope you can find a place to live near here so you can keep coming to this school," I responded.

"We're looking for a house in the country. I'm going to keep coming to this school because my mom graduated from here. It's a tradition."

"Oh, that's good. I'm glad you'll be able to stay with your friends and teachers."

Another student, a boy, raised his hand and I called on him. "Officer Potter, I can't give money for the Hurricane Katrina fund because my father says we need it to pay for gas for our car. He says a lot of people are hurting, trying to find money for gasoline."

"That's right. It's okay to use your money for your family. Not everyone can give money right now to those who are homeless."

Then I called on a girl, Brandy, I didn't know very well. She looked pretty serious. *"Was there a problem?"* I wondered.

"Officer Potter, is our school safe?"

While I like to think I'm ready for about any question a grade school student may ask, I'm still occasionally surprised, marveling at the thought process of young children. The question about safety at school was such a general question that I needed to find out what motivated her to ask it. Was she thinking about her bicycle being stolen, a bully in the bathroom or an armed intruder shooting children?

School is very safe, but accidents and crimes are well documented. No matter how many signs are posted outside school buildings across the country, there are still drugs, guns or violence inside too many of our educational establishments.

"I can tell you, Brandy, school is the safest place for children. It's safer than when you're playing outside in your neighborhood or when you're home alone after school. With all the adult supervision at school you're very secure. But why do you ask the question? Can you give me an example of what you're thinking that might be dangerous or make you feel unsafe? If you can, then I might be able to give you a better answer."

Brandy explained, "I saw on a movie last night where a boy brought a gun into his classroom. He shot a girl because he was mad at her. Is our school safe from that happening?"

Never before had I been asked such a hard question from someone so young. I'd been asked if I had ever watched someone die but that seemed to be more about the questioner's curiosity than any personal fear. This question sounded like the type of inquiry every principal, board member or school security officer should pose every single day as part of their ongoing effort to reduce opportunities for deadly violence. In my ideal world, children shouldn't have to ask a life and death question about their school.

"Brandy, I can't promise that a gun will never be brought into your school by an angry classmate. I can tell you that keeping that from happening is a team effort of everyone at our school and in the community. It means parents and guardians get involved in the lives of their children before a crisis occurs. The boy that shot the girl didn't understand that when he got angry there were nonviolent ways of dealing with the problem. Adults need to teach children skills for solving conflicts plus they need to keep firearms locked up when not in use because small children don't understand the deadly results they can cause.

"Children can also help in making their schools a safer place by treating each other fairly and letting adults know when they need help solving problems.

"What's one thing you can do to help make your school safer?" I asked.

"You mentioned treating others fairly," Brandy replied. "Treating others the way you want to be treated is called the Golden Rule."

"Oh, yes! If we all practiced that rule then we wouldn't have people hurting one another," I agreed.

"Another thing to remember is that if you ever see someone with a weapon at school you need to tell your teacher. Sometimes students know when a friend brings a gun to school, but they don't tell an adult. Telling an adult right away could help save someone's life. Remember to never bring a gun to school. We don't want people to be hurt.

"Now, I'm going to share with you some information about bicycle safety. The first thing to remember is that sometimes people driving cars and trucks have trouble seeing you when you're on your bicycle. Just because you see them doesn't mean they see you. Also, once they see you it doesn't mean that they can stop fast enough to keep from hitting you. You've got to be extra careful when you're out riding your bike. Follow the safety rules that your parents or caregivers have set for you."

* * *

After my presentation the teacher asked if I had time to go to recess with her class. When I said, "Yes, I'd love to" the children were excited and even cheered. *"What a job I've got,"*   I thought, then thanked God for my good fortune. Who, besides teachers get paid for going to recess?

I was immediately in demand as one girl asked me to push her on a swing, a boy wanted to know if I'd play tag with him and his friends, and the teacher, on our way outside, told me that hearing her children share their economic challenges always made her feel more empathetic for them. Then, unexpectedly, considering the circumstances of transitioning to the playground she asked me, "So, how safe is our school? Do you think it could happen here?"

"The short answer is yes. It could happen in any classroom in any school. That's scary, I know. Fortunately, most children don't have the combination of skill, will, and availability of a weapon, all at the same time. Since schools, especially at the elementary level, represent childhood and innocence we don't make the buildings armed fortresses. Most don't have security guards or metal detectors. As long as we continue to allow so much freedom of movement in and around our schools the opportunity to do harm is great. But we can do better.

"School boards won't want to hear this, but for our country to really have safer schools we need armed security at every single one. And security is more than a uniform and a radio—it means having trained, armed personnel ready to protect and save the lives of children and staff by being prepared to use deadly force if and when necessary.[47]

"I've been discussing school safety plans a lot lately with the school district administrators," I continued. "We're attempting to make sure that the procedures for intruders and bomb threats are in place and that the employees and students are clear about what action to take upon notification of these emergencies. Once the school is as prepared for threats of violence from people as they are for threats from accidents and the weather, we'll be reducing our risks of injury and death considerably."

While watching a group of students on the new playground equipment she asked me, "What can we do?"

"Let's take your school for example. The chain link fence around this playground is a tremendous help for psychologically and physically protecting the children. Keeping the doors to the school locked except for the main door by the office is another best practice for school safety. We also need parents and guardians to understand why certain things are done. We want them to feel welcome to visit their school, but they need to understand that a procedure of checking into the office makes the school campus safer for their children. Teachers and staff need to be trained like sales people in retail, to greet the visitor and to ask how they may help them. More and more schools require visitors to sign in and obtain a visitor pass to wear. This is all part of knowing and controlling who is in our school. These procedures won't stop all intruders and they won't prevent a child from bringing a gun to school, but they are just a few of the many steps that make a campus more secure."

* * *

Later in the day, during the upcoming lunch period I had planned on surprising the second grade by sitting at their designated table. Instead, I got an offer I couldn't refuse. The principal asked me to join a group of the teachers in the teacher's lounge. She told me that my visit in the morning had sparked some questions from teachers about what to do in an emergency if an angry, out-of control parent showed up at the office or at the door of a teacher's classroom.

Watching the teachers' fast-paced eating reminded me of sheriff's deputies, focusing on getting their meal down as quickly as possible while eating at a restaurant, fearful of the next telephone call, page or transmission on the walkie-talkie, knowing it might require a quick exit. The principal and I continued our conversation as we sat down and the few teachers that had been talking, gradually stopped and listened to our conversation.

"As long as you have an intercom system," I shared, "any teacher or staff should have the authority to put the school into a lockdown procedure and call 911 to have law enforcement alerted to respond immediately. Once the lockdown is announced, either by the secretary, principal, custodian or a teacher, everyone should gather their students into the classroom and lock their doors as soon as possible. The teachers should turn off the lights, have everyone get out of sight and take roll. Until the school administrator or law enforcement advises differently, the teachers should keep their rooms secured."

Mr. Northrup, who reminded me of Mr. Rogers of TV fame, was the only male classroom teacher at the school. He jumped into the conversation. "I didn't hear the first part of your advice, but if an intruder comes into our school, what should I do if one of my students is in the bathroom down the hall? Should I leave my other students to find the one outside the classroom?"

"These are hard questions especially because they could involve life and death. Our plans are not perfect, but we're not advising teachers to leave the classroom once a lockdown has been established. You can go to the door and visually check the hallway for any students. You may want to urge any students that are nearby into your classroom before locking the door. We're hoping that with practice, students will learn that an announcement of the lockdown procedure means to get back to their class or any classroom immediately. If there's time in the lockdown, those staff members that don't have a classroom of students, like custodians, may have an opportunity to check the hallways and bathrooms depending on the nature of the lockdown. Like I said earlier, we'll want all the teachers to promptly take roll so they'll know if they're missing any students. Once you're locked down then stay that way until contacted by your administration or law enforcement.

Another teacher, a half-eaten apple in her hand spoke up, "How safe are our rooms?"

"I wish they were safer, but your rooms are better than the hallways or a commons area. To the aggressor out-of-site is often out of mind. Whether the intruder is an irate parent or an armed student your quick action by locking the door can prevent or help delay a possible confrontation, injury or death. At the same time the barriers will give law enforcement valuable time to muster troops to the scene."

Mrs. Davis, petite but with a survivor's mentality, spoke next. "This may sound crazy but can I have pepper spray in case the intruder tries to break into my room?"

"I'm not sure what the law is on that. You know you're not allowed to have a firearm on school property. But I like your thinking. I know we don't want a bunch of potential weapons in everyone's classrooms, but in the case of life and death I'd be thinking ahead of time on how to protect myself if it came down to any person trying to break into my classroom. Depending on your room's layout, could your desk and tables be used to help block the doorway or at least the small window in the door?"

"We're going to need to end this conversation shortly," the principal advised me, looking at her watch. She seemed a bit uncomfortable.

"I appreciate you taking the time to think about this unpleasant possibility," I concluded. "I call it imagining the unimaginable. We all hope that we'll never need to lockdown the school, but we need the crisis plan, we need everyone to know how to respond and we need for everyone to practice it."

Then I heard from a teacher recognized for her success in the classroom. Her class regularly excelled in state standards in reading and math. "We have a few other things to do, like making sure our assessments continue to improve, Sergeant Potter. Have you heard of No Child Left Behind?"

"Yes, I've heard about it and I try and appreciate the pressure you're under to show adequate yearly progress so you're not labeled a school in need of improvement. But to me No Child Left Behind has another meaning. It means that none of our children should be left behind when an intruder enters the building with the intent of hurting one of them. We can't protect all the children when they're out of school but we have the obligation to do all we can once they come to this sanctuary. Is my thinking faulty, to strive for academic achievement in an environment that's safe?

"You practice fire drills and tornado drills regularly even though I've never known your school to have a fire or to suffer any tornado damage. Practicing for an intruder will take some time away from studying, but while you're in a lockdown, for drill or for real, you can still have class. I'll bet that with your proven leadership abilities, you could have your students estimating the amount of time it takes for them to get to their safer positions. Or, with the class sitting on the floor, out-of-site, you could quietly read them a chapter from a favorite book. Remember that the children will take their cues from you about how to respond in times of a potential crisis. If you take it seriously yet calmly, so will they. A few practice drills doesn't need to derail your teaching opportunities."

Then the principal spoke up as the teachers gathered their trays and tossed their garbage. "Sgt. Potter, thanks for being willing to visit with us about intruders. We'll get back with you as we prepare for our first armed intruder drill, but first we have to survive next week's assessments."

30

ROLE MODEL MATERIAL

"HOW DO YOU SELECT THE BEST SCHOOL RESOURCE OFFICER?"

"No two students are exactly alike except that they're counting on you."
—Public Broadcasting System advertisement

R are is the law enforcement agency that selects a poor school resource officer. Some reasons for this success are that, for one, the agencies I'm familiar with all ask for officers who are genuinely interested to apply for the position. That prevents the special assignment from being forcibly filled by a screaming, scared macho man, who would rather be in a car chase, shoot out, or working a solitary beat on a slow night shift, than traversing a miniature city of children, where each shadowy silhouette is seen as an untested encounter as risky as a "routine" traffic stop. Also, the departmental interview panel for finding the right full-time SRO often includes an educator, usually the school principal, and sometimes a school counselor, who have their own ideas of what personality traits are necessary for helping them maintain an environment most conducive to learning. They're also aware that the officer they select must have the communication skills to keep them abreast of the changing school climate.

In the SRO interviews I've been a part of, there are as many factors for the officer wanting the assignment as there are abilities to do the job well. Some applicants simply want out of what they are presently doing, as soon as possible. This could be from job burnout where the employee needs a change of environment or duties. For example, when I left patrol for the schools, I knew I wouldn't miss the fatality wrecks or working rotating shifts. A challenge for the interviewer is to predict if someone that is running away from something, not running to something, will have the commitment for the work.

I remember when I was helping interview perspective SROs. One interviewee answered that she desired to be an SRO because she had always felt that her creator had put her here to make a difference and that helping enrich children's lives was part of this spiritual journey. When she shared this very personal passion for the job it made all the difference in helping her stand out from the other candidates. Our interviewers approved of her belief system and appreciated her candor. In another culture, or simply a different group of interview board members, sharing a spiritual revelation might have been considered inappropriate and too personal.

Another inspiring officer, from his very first police department interview, told the board he "wanted to work with kids and have an influence in their lives."[48]   Sure enough, as an SRO he helped change lives for the better by first recognizing how important they were. He also realized how fortunate he was, to be able to work with the children on a daily basis in his school assignment, rather than the brief time he had to interact with people while taking reports on patrol.[49]

What character traits are important in an SRO? Whether officers are working traditional law enforcement assignments or helping children develop into responsible citizens, they need more than drive and direction. They must possess common sense. Since SROs are often working their own schedule, they are also required to be self-motivated, trustworthy, and dependable. Liking people, especially the ability to easily interact with children, is a must. There's a saying that an insincere person can fool everyone but children and dogs. While there are always exceptions to that adage, the evaluation from a school's youthful population about their officer's integrity, or lack of it, might compete favorably to a well-administered polygraph exam.

It's a given that any officer constantly around children, especially once rapport has been developed, will become a role model to juveniles. Because of this access to maturing minds, an agency has a monumental responsibility to recognize how much an applicant's personal habits and traits of character count. This examination may even include an officer's use of legal drugs and that means alcohol and tobacco.

We've asked candidates if they drink or smoke. If they do partake then they're questioned about how much and how often they use. While it may seem personal or immaterial if a potential SRO uses tobacco or not, we are asking the question before the students do. We know that children will mimic their elders, especially those closest to them. If an SRO smokes or chews tobacco then the drug that's legal for the officer will be more acceptable to a multitude of potential underage customers. Wouldn't it be a crime to have an SRO teach formal lessons about making healthy decisions but to be known personally by his or her students for being unable to "just say no"?

One officer that understood the importance of a private life away from legal drugs had an outstanding interview. He talked about his schooling, experience, and when asked about his belief about drugs, spoke of his former life in the military, where smoking and drinking surrounded him for a period of time. He said that like any other sailor, he believed it was his duty to drink as much alcohol as was available at the time. He smoked back then too, despite knowing the risks. Having personally changed his lifestyle years prior to applying for the SRO position, and conveying his then current substance free standards so well, made the interview staff confident he could communicate the same message to children. After all, our purpose is not to portray our officers in the schools as perfect or without problems. It's to help the youth understand that sometimes it takes a lot of determination, even struggle, to continue to work on improving oneself every day.

I've known SROs from other agencies who began their job assignment as a smoker, thinking they could keep this personal matter a secret from their students. My how we deceive ourselves for our addictions! All the mouthwash or air spray that can fit in an officer's Crown Vic, Chevy Impala, or Dodge Intrepid, can't fool a class of kids, especially when the youngest demand their hugs. They know when you smell like one of their cigarette-smoking parents or guardians.

Bad grammar is another element that surfaces unintentionally during an interview. As an applicant is talking about his or her traits and skills that make them a desirable candidate they sometimes reveal more than they realize. After all, you can't keep your mouth shut in interviews or classroom visits—you must talk. I've known grade school teachers who tell law enforcement administrators that they simply won't have a particular officer back in their classroom. After the teacher has explained for weeks or months the necessity of proper grammar in the workplace, and a visiting officer repeatedly demonstrates how many times he can use "ain't" in his conversation, there is conflict in the classroom. This is another example of the mixed messages our children sometimes receive. If the slang is in the student's home, teachers have no control and they know it, but if it's in their classroom, they will treat the intruder as an unwelcome weed in their precious garden. It must be pulled and banished from the garden plot. We all have our standards.

Even though I've mentioned the basic

requirement of common sense, that's not the same thing as thinking creatively on your feet. One of the biggest surprises in D.A.R.E.® and SRO basic trainings is when you're asked to come to the front of the room and stand before your peers. Then you're instructed to perform spontaneously by talking for two minutes about a particular single word (toe, rock, paradigm, etc.) chosen from a stack of shuffled index cards. The experience is sobering.

Thinking clearly and quickly can really impress that panel of people who are deciding on the best officer for the SRO slot. But failing to perform well might also be helpful. It can favorably impact the officer to always be prepared for any future lesson so that she will never again have to feel the embarrassment of fumbling for words.

I've seen officers publicly melt down during those two minutes as though they were just given a life sentence term in prison. At my D.A.R.E.® officer training in Springfield, Illinois, I recall standing before the room full of officers and being assigned the word *cow*. As my mind raced for things to say I found myself revealing my personal life, especially my vegan eating philosophy with its limited dietary choices and how cow's milk is healthiest when consumed by calves, not human adults. When the facilitator said, "Time," I was glad I hadn't murdered anyone in my past or I might have confessed to that too, because of the highly uncomfortable circumstances. If only our detectives could replicate these stressful conditions for future suspect interviews, we would have more confessions.

My favorite memory of the meltdown activity

was in SRO training when an officer was given the word *paradigm*. It was quickly evident that he had no concept of the word so he began to talk about a pair-of-dimes! In no time at all he was advising us how two dimes could be exchanged for four nickels and what we could buy for twenty cents. Even as I belly laughed at his predicament I knew it could have been me up there on the spot.

The best impromptu presentation I've ever observed was in an interview with a ranking officer who kept the panel spellbound. In his few seconds of preparation time he ripped a sheet of paper from his notebook and announced to the three-person panel that he was going to teach us how to build and fly a paper airplane. With his prop in hand he had our undivided attention. He then proceeded, step by step, to show us where, why, and how to fold the construction paper. After heavily creasing each wing of his remarkably precise little airplane, he tapped the nose to the table top...weighing it just right with just the right touch.

But would it fly? Confident to the very end, this speaker took the plane, cocked back his hand, and released it in the interview room. As the projectile caught the air it lofted up, deftly defying gravity, making a dramatic flight past the heads of the spellbound, child-like panelists. As the airplane skidded to a landing the two-minute buzzer sounded. We were in awe! Spontaneously, inspirationally appreciative of his performance, we applauded!

That's the kind of officer we wanted in our schools!

31

Rules and Rudeness

"DOES ROSALIE UNDERSTAND CAUSE AND EFFECT?"

"Wisdom begins when you realize there are other points of view."
—Unknown Author

I'd been invited back for my third visit of the school year to examine conflict resolution. When I called the day before to see if there was a specific timely topic, the teacher had remarked, "The students still get an attitude when they feel they've been wronged and want to get back at the other person. Sometimes I don't know if I've made any progress with them."

This attitude she referred to didn't seem to me to be solely a concern of her high school students with special educational needs. Wasn't nearly everyone in our country, possibly world, exposed on a daily basis to this "eye for an eye" mentality of problem solving? Was it a surprise that getting even was seemingly a universal sign of strength, not weakness? One need only read the front page of any major newspaper to understand how the drama in the world was a blueprint, a model, for many of our young people to see violence as the solution to their problems.

* * *

As I entered the classroom and looked for familiar faces I was not disappointed. Rosalie was present and I greeted her warmly. She was a favorite from my first visit. Her eyes were always watchful and penetrating. Her mind always active. Since I was still trying to figure her out this was another opportunity to gather more information about her.

I recalled that she found strength by winning arguments and was even prepared to get physical to defend herself. She was a survivor with a set of her own rules. She had explained to me previously that getting in a fight prevented further problems with individuals. The challenger "had been taught a lesson," she would say.

Rosalie, like many of her classmates, had displayed engaging intelligence and the drive to seek answers to those things that were important to her. One thing she couldn't quite understand was why everyone else, especially her boyfriend, didn't see as clearly as she did when they were wrong. Why, when she could prove something, was there still denial? Was it that they just didn't want to admit to being mistaken or was it an inability to understand cause and effect?

* * *

Rosalie didn't want to know if my gun was loaded or details of any dangerous police car chase. Instead she wanted to know why there were senseless rules.

"Sgt. Potter, I was in a car with friends at three in the morning and we were stopped by a cop for doing nothing wrong."

"Were you stopped in town?" I asked.

"Yes, but we weren't doing anything wrong."

"Are you eighteen yet?" I continued.

"Almost, I'm seventeen."

"I don't know what got the officer's attention for the traffic stop, but there's a midnight curfew within the city limits for those under eighteen."

"But why is there a rule like that? We weren't doing anything wrong and the cop was rude to us."

"How about using drugs or alcohol?" I automatically inquired, already jumping to conclusions, looking for balance to the story.

After Rosalie said no with her whole body, I agreed that most young people don't break the law, but I explained that a curfew prevented some problems from occurring, especially in the middle of the night. Her verbal and non-verbal response to me had been echoed time and again by others, generation after generation of young people...there's nothing to do, we just wanted to socialize, there was no place to be but in the car and we were targeted unfairly for being young.

"Even though you don't feel like you were doing anything wrong and you don't agree with the curfew ordinance, being out at three in the morning invited the officer to do the obvious... enforce the law. What did he do that was rude?"

"It was the way he treated us. My mother wouldn't answer the door when he brought me home. She slammed the door in his face."

I was getting confused, recognizing that my career as a cop tended to show a favorable bias towards the law enforcement officer. It seemed to me, from my perspective, that when the officer brought Rosalie safely home to her mother he might have been anticipating at least civility, if not cooperation. It sure sounded to me as though he was being blamed for Rosalie's actions. I could understand Rosalie being upset, but failed at comprehending her mother's thinking.

"Rosalie," I said, "Why did your mother react that way?"

Rosalie was silent.

"The officer brought you home safe," I continued.

She thought about it another moment then chose to include me in the reality of her world.

"I take care of myself and my mother. She doesn't take care of me."

* * *

There was no point, since I wasn't on the 3 a.m. traffic stop to determine who was rude to whom. It might have been the officer setting the tone for conflict, using his authoritarian voice, scolding both Rosalie and her mother like bad little children. Considering how similar some officers' personalities were to Rosalie's, the two individuals might have easily clashed. Officers like to be right. We like to be in control. We don't like to be told what to do. In essence, we detest being treated as powerless children, yet that's exactly how we can treat others when they make mistakes.

I could just imagine Rosalie telling the biggest and the "baddest" copper that she and her friends weren't doing anything wrong! And she probably believed it because in her mind the curfew law was unjust. It wasn't her law and she had never agreed to abide by it. She was unwilling to compromise with anyone when she thought she was right, which was probably the reason I liked her so easily. She had her own distinct standards or rules and she lived by them. They just weren't the same ones that her boyfriend, the school and the city had in place.

* * *

"Rosalie, whether you agree with a rule or not, there are consequences when you choose to break them. For example, what do you think could happen if a person forgets to set her alarm clock to get up in time for school or work?"

"She might not wake up in time to get to school."

"And if she was late very often then what could happen?"

"She could get fired or receive a Saturday detention."

"If an employee is late for work, is that a good time to argue with the boss about the starting time being so early?"

"Well, if it's too early then that could be a reason for being late. I don't have an alarm clock."

"Oh. My point is that if you're caught outside past curfew, then arguing about the ordinance when you're caught doesn't help you. Remember officers enforce the laws; they don't make them.

Same thing with speeding—arguing about the posted speed limit when you're caught speeding is just a waste of time. In fact, disagreeing with an officer face-to-face on the street can easily escalate to further problems, especially if you're rude. If you want to disagree then disagree in court. Plead not guilty."

"What if they're rude first?"

"I'm trying to get you to understand your odds—to predict what will happen when you make a particular choice." I was beginning to grasp that this was a bigger problem than just giving Rosalie a few tips on thinking ahead and considering her options.

* * *

I reviewed the information she had given me. In the same way Rosalie would present evidence to her boyfriend when she knew he was wrong, the officer could prove Rosalie was breaking the law. But in this case Rosalie couldn't see it because in her mind the law was irrelevant—even nonexistent. What was that ancient Tibetan saying? "I have eyes to see you. I need a mirror to see myself." I could sense a self-righteous attitude in Rosalie towards anyone, especially the police, when she would proclaim, "I'm right. You're wrong. I'll do what I want to do. If I'm caught, then I'll debate the law and attack the other person." (Sounded like an attorney with a weak case.)

If only Rosalie could trade in her argumentative and aggressive interactions for assertiveness (standing up for her rights while still respecting the rights of others) then she would be one powerful force. If she could learn to perceive others as less hostile and develop better interactive skills then I believed she would drastically increase her positive outcomes in situations that were potentially confrontational.

* * *

"Rosalie, when you get mad at someone, what do you do?"

"I might yell at them. It depends."

"Good. Being able to figure out when it's appropriate to yell is a big step in keeping things from getting worse. I can tell that you like to give your opinion on things. In fact, I think your ability to debate is a trait that can help you succeed. Maybe someday you'll have your own talk show, be an attorney, or a police officer."

"Police officer?!"

"Sure! You're willing to fight for what you believe is right. Occasionally officers have to fight to protect themselves and others. But our goal is to control the situation without force whenever possible. We prefer to be assertive rather than aggressive."

I acknowledge the silence. The class waits for me to continue.

"Rosalie, are you willing to help me out in a role play for the class?"

"Maybe. What do I have to do?"

"We're going to act out a situation on the street—just you and me. It's practice."

"Okay," she agrees without making the slightest move from her chair.

Before I give further instructions I continue thinking about Rosalie's readiness at a young seventeen to disagree with a uniformed police officer. This reminds me of the saying about the fight in the dog being more important than its size. Rosalie has both.

"Rosalie, we're going to pretend that you're a professional, polite, police officer doing her job when a teenager (that will be me) is out past curfew. As you're driving your patrol car some how I catch your attention. What am I doing that you notice?"

She answers, "Speeding," then proceeds to the front of the classroom, standing next to me. Rosalie's getting into character. She's not popping her knuckles, but I detect some flexing of shoulder muscles

"Okay. I'm speeding and you pull me over. Now, it's up to you to show the class how to handle this traffic stop in a respectful manner."

"Should I start now?"

"Just a second." I grab a nearby chair, pull it over and sit down. I place my hands as if I'm gripping a steering wheel, then with my left hand I pretend to roll down my window.

"Why are you cops always picking on me? I didn't do anything wrong!" I yell defiantly.

Officer Rosalie's mouth drops open in surprise. She doesn't speak. I can't wait for her reply.

Finally, she says, "Did you know there's a curfew law in Hutchinson?"

"But I didn't do anything wrong!"

"Even though the curfew law isn't fair to high school students who are practically adults it's still the law," replies Officer Rosalie.

"But why is there such a stupid rule?" I ask.

"Because adults like to tell teenagers what to do...and it's for your safety."

I smile. Rosalie may not believe in curfew ordinances but I've just heard her give a reason why they exist. We're making progress. Her thinking needs to change before her behavior can follow.

"Great job, Rosalie! How about it class? Give it up for Officer Rosalie!"

The class of eight or nine students applauds while a boy waves his hand and asks, "Can I go next?"

"Rosalie, before you sit down I've got to ask you a question. How were you able to stay in control when I started off yelling that you were picking on me and that it wasn't fair you stopped me? Wasn't that disrespectful?"

Her answer is a lesson for me.

"I didn't see it that way. Your loud voice and complaining didn't bother me. You were just talkin'."

"Oh. Okay. We do see things differently. In the house where I grew up, I thought yelling was a sign of disrespect—not just loud conversation. You've just expanded my thinking by showing me another way to interpret people's behavior."

32

YOUTH CAMP

"DO YOU TRUST ME?"

"Teachers open the door, but you must enter by yourself."
—Chinese Proverb

It was already hot. After months of planning, meeting after meeting, fund raising, recruiting counselors, scheduling speakers, planning and purchasing food, and ordering tee-shirts, we were minutes away from loading buses for the Sheriff's Department annual summer Youth Camp. Kids, parents and caregivers of all shapes and sizes, with their colorful collection of clothing and mixed emotions, had gathered next to the carefully cleaned school buses, filling the air with anticipation and wonder.

As the clock ticked closer to our hour of departure I again checked the table by the stack of schedules and maps. There were still three name tags remaining. I had a minute to speculate if the kids were coming or not, but as long as we had our bus drivers I knew that we weren't waiting one additional moment for stragglers. One thought was clear, *"The unstoppable show had begun."* Instead of sharing that insight, I announced with a megaphone the final group goodbye, "It's time to give your loved ones a hug and a kiss before loading the buses." This was met with a mixture of laughter, shrieks and groans. Then I watched as the adults and children showed different levels of comfort and discomfort before the children broke away, hurrying for a friend or acquaintance, then to a bus and a seat.

Counselors stationed at each bus's entrance were armed with a clipboard, camp roster and pencil. The price of admittance on the bus was a personalized name tag. After marking the list and checking it twice we brought the clipboards together to find out whose names were not checked off. Our procedure confirmed that three students who had previously planned on attending and who had made no alternate travel arrangements with us, were nowhere in sight. On this final note we gave the thumbs up signal to the bus drivers to start their engines.

Slowly the reptilian caravan began, first turtle-like then as a snake weaving its way through the parking lot and Hutchinson streets until we were headed westward on state highway K-96. Once the string of vehicles was progressing safely down the highway toward the campground I reviewed the roster so that I could begin to investigate the circumstances of our non-campers. After checking the phone number my first call was to one of "my" kids, meaning he was from one of the schools where I taught classes. His name was Alex.

Any number of things could have delayed a camper from getting to the buses on time, but I wanted to hear the reason first hand for the no-show status, and also to see if the child would or would not be arriving late to camp. When Alex didn't arrive in time for the bus ride I was really disappointed because his mother had told me on a couple of occasions how excited he was going off to camp for the first time in his life. As our entourage slowed, approaching Nickerson, I was glad to have Alex's mom answer the phone on my first attempt.

"Mrs. Douglas, this is Sgt. Potter with the Sheriff's Department on our way to camp with the buses. Is everything okay? Has there been an emergency?"

"Alex has his bags packed, but he won't go."

"What's wrong?"

"I don't know for sure. He won't get in the car. I think he's scared."

"Has he stayed away from home overnight before?"

"One time at a friend's house, that's all."

"May I speak with him? If I convince him to go to camp can you get him there? Do you have the map with directions we sent in the mail?"

"Oh, you're welcome to talk to him. I don't know if it'll do any good. I've tried everything. He's sitting right here. Yes, I have the map and schedule, but I don't know if I have enough gas in the car. I'll put him on."

"...hello...?"

"Hello, Alex! How are you doing?"

"Fine."

"We missed you at the sports arena."

"I forgot about camp."

"What? No one forgets about Youth Camp! Your mom told me you've been excited about it."

"I overslept."

"Overslept! It's past noon on camp day! No

one oversleeps on camp day! Your mom can take you to camp right now and we'll meet you there. You won't miss a thing."

"I'm going to do stuff here."

"What? What are you going to do that's more exciting than a weekend at camp?"

"We might go fishing."

"Listen, we have a weekend planned that's full of fun! It will be a blast! We have swimming, horseback riding, water games, a campfire with s'mores, a ventriloquist, magician, musicians and even free time."

"...yeah."

"Do you like to swim?"

"Yeah."

"Alex, do you like to eat?"

"Yeah."

"Well, we have more food than you could possibly eat! Camp will be so much fun, you just need to get there to find out."

"I can't go."

"What do you mean you can't? Your mom says she'll take you. Do you want to go?"

"Yeah, I want to go."

"Then throw your bags in the car and Mom will drive you to camp."

"I just can't."

"Alex, you're scared of going aren't you?"

"No, I'm not scared."

"You are too. It's okay to be scared of something you've never done before. That's normal. This is a big opportunity for you that I don't want you to miss. Remember in class we talked about healthy and unhealthy risks that people take? This is one of those healthy risks that when you take it, you will grow as a person."

"I want to, but I can't."

"Alex, listen to me. Do you trust me?"

"Yes."

"Then take this risk. I wouldn't be recommending you to do this if I felt it was unsafe. I'll be there and there will be plenty of counselors to look out for you. This is a healthy risk worth taking. It will give you an experience to help you in your future. You still plan on playing professional football, don't you?"

"Yes."

"I've got news for you. Not all of their games are home games! They play out of town too. Getting away from home is something that you can gradually get used to doing. You can start now. Camp is a safe opportunity for you to take a small step towards being away from home overnight. So, will you go?"

"...I can't."

"Put your mom back on."

"Hello," said Mrs. Douglas.

"It sounds like he's scared of going," I agreed.

"I'll pick him up and carry him to the car!" threatened Mrs. Douglas, making me laugh. At age twelve he was a head taller than his mother and solid as a boulder.

"No. If he won't go voluntarily then I wouldn't make him. It's a shame he won't take this healthy risk of being away from home. This would really be good for him. He could have so much fun! Let me ask you this though, do you want him to go?"

"Of course I do. This is something the two of us have been talking about," explained Alex's mother.

"Well, the reason I ask is that sometimes the parents, especially single parents like you, are having mixed feelings about their child leaving. The kids may pick up on this feeling."

"I do want him to go. It would be good for him."

"Okay. I was just checking. Put Alex back on for a minute."

"...hello."

"Okay, Alex, I can understand that you're reluctant to leave home where you're safe and to go somewhere you've never been. If you're also thinking about how this is like abandoning your mom, it's not! It doesn't mean you don't love your mother. She's not kicking you out of the house and you're not abandoning her. This is only for the weekend! She wants you to grow up and be successful. This is an early step with you becoming comfortable with yourself and with being away from home. This is also a step toward becoming a professional athlete. Since I know how much you care about your mother, remember that when you help yourself you're helping her too. This can be practice for an overnight, out-of-town game."

"I can't."

"Okay. It's your choice. No one can make you go. If you change your mind you're welcome to show up. I've got to make a couple more calls. Have fun."

"Goodbye."

I was surprised! I had absolutely believed I could talk Alex into going to camp, that at any moment he would tell me that he had changed his mind. I didn't have anymore time for him, though. There were others that mattered too.

For me, in years past, the peaceful drive to camp was an opportunity to have a meditative moment, to collect my thoughts and enjoy the scenery. Not any more. This year, since I had borrowed a departmental cell phone for the weekend, I was discovering how helpful it could be for better communication. I was especially glad after my calls to know the up-to-date status of the three no-show campers. This allowed us to know the magic number—ninety-two. That was how many young students we would have at camp. I also knew from experience that as the weekend progressed the number would likely decline by a few, not necessarily due to physical ailments but to the emotional turmoil prevalent in adolescents when they are hit by homesickness. The ailment would peak tomorrow afternoon or evening around the end of Family Day after an afternoon of fun and games, when the adults prepared to return home—without their camper. But as our group of vehicles approached the campground I took care of my immediate needs, eating a banana, drinking more water and applying a heavy dose of sunscreen.

Upon arriving at camp we went on a tour of the grounds, then everyone grabbed a bunk. After that, it was time for free time activities like basketball, swimming or horseback riding. It was then, while I was helping bring up gear from the basement of the dinning hall that I was informed that someone was upstairs looking for me. I thought, *"It's awfully early for this evening's speaker to be here, but who else could it be?"* To my total shock, as I rounded the corner from the stairs, there stood Alex

Douglas! He was beaming, just as proud of himself as he could be, taller and more broad shouldered than I had remembered. Behind him with a smirk of a smile nearly as wide as his, was his mother. Like a cheerleader I started yelling! "Alex! You did it! Way to go!" We were both so thrilled that we hugged. This was a milestone!

When I walked Mrs. Douglas to her car she told me that she thought Alex was fine and would stay the weekend. I was so happy he had arrived that any early departure was the least of my concerns. As Mrs. Douglas opened her car door she told me she would be back the following afternoon for Family Day. Then she looked up and the sun caught her eyes. A luminous tear, like a drop of rain on a window, progressed down her face. I didn't know if it was a tear of joy for her son's courage, fear of losing him or both.

As Mrs. Douglas drove away I walked Alex to a bunk house, helped him carry his gear in and made sure he found a bed. For much of the remaining afternoon he was hesitant about going off on his own and ended up helping counselors fill water balloons. Gradually, though, he seemed to blend into the rhythm of his peers.

He survived the night. His mother showed up early for Family Day and the twosome stayed pretty close to one another during the fire hose soccer game, the slippery soapy tug-of-war and the water balloon launches. I lost track of them for awhile but they told me how much they enjoyed the picnic. Next thing I knew I saw them sitting together at the beginning of the talent show.

During the show Alex approached me. "I've decided to go home with my mother," he told me directly face to face, on his own with no adult intermediary.

"You do whatever you feel is right for you. Alex, I'm proud of you for taking the risk. Thanks for coming to camp."

EMOTIONAL CONNECTIONS

"DO WE MAKE A DIFFERENCE?"

"407, Dispatch."
"Dispatch, 407, go ahead."
"Request juvenile detective 10-43 me at my 10-42 reference a child sexual abuse case. R.P. (reporting party) is standing by."
"10-4, 407. Will advise."

———————

One thing I've learned in my life, made clearer to me after working with young people for so long, is that we are here to uplift one another along the path of life. We all make a difference. We're all connected. It's just that we don't always get to know what that connection might be.

This past year I had a retiring school superintendent thank me for my years of service helping educate students. Then he asked me if I ever got discouraged with the continuing problems of drugs and violence.

"Maybe I've lowered the bar," I admitted. "I no longer believe I will influence everyone, but I still believe I can influence someone. It's up to them."

Soon after graduating from college I had the conviction that as a prison volunteer, grade school teacher and security officer I would change the world. I'd do this through my strong values of faith, determination and a passion for the work. But after several years on the job as an officer—on the road and in the schools—it became obvious to me that locally and nationally, statistics of drug use and violence fluctuate year to year. This caused me to reevaluate my influence.

I learned to be modest in my expectations, especially when it involved other people's behavior. If I took credit for a success then wasn't it fair for me to be blamed for the negative results as well? It was an awkward position. I viewed it as similar to the predicament many parents face when they raise two children and one gets into serious trouble. When that occurs are they perpetually prone to feel self-doubt about anything positive they've done in the process of their child-rearing and parenting? Do they forever feel like failures even though at an early age individuals make their own choices? Who's to say that without the loving guidance of the parents, the children would have been in much worse trouble? Parents always receive my vote as being the most influential people in a child's life. Who else has so much personal contact with young children?

Some people believe that police officers, just because we have a badge and a gun, can influence children to do anything. In reality, our intimidation factor is generally of short duration. Our expandable baton is not a magic wand! What really makes a difference, what resonates with children, is an open heart and a determination to find a way to be part of their lives. Once this happens it takes an ability to explain why something is important, a continual willingness to listen and the ongoing capacity to teach useful strategies for learning.

I still remember when law enforcement in our county first decided to allocate resources for one officer to participate fulltime in our handfull of school districts. It was a giant step, a leap of faith. It led to politicians, principals and parents encouraging us to get more deeply involved because with our influence, it was hoped we could help stem the tide of unhealthy behaviors.

As uniformed visitors on an educational mission we were welcomed into the local schools. Administrators understood that a partnership with police officers would tap into an under used resource—the prevention side of the police. Behind the body armor or "bullet proof vest" was the human side, where children learned that the officer could become a trusted friend, not a person to fear. In no time at all strong relationships blossomed.

* * *

"Dispatch, 407, juvenile detective in route."
The radio traffic I might have overheard on my scanner only scratched the surface of an inspiring story. A fellow officer had been sought out by one of his D.A.R.E.® students from the previous school year. She was desperate. She was looking for safety after years of abuse from a step-father, an ex-convict who would return to prison. When she made the bold, deeply personal decision to seek help, it was the person behind the badge she trusted and turned to.

The very young teen sought her school officer at his home. When the door bell rang he answered. It's just another example that there are times when police officers may not be *on* duty, but they're never *off* duty.

When the victim of abuse reached out for help and it was given, it reinforced my belief that we really do help change the world one person—one moment—at a time. I was also reminded about the best conditions for young people to undergo a spurt in their growth, a transformational moment. When there is a deep connection with others combined with a profound need for change then good things happen. Both were present when the girl made her disclosure.

There are obvious, memorable times when a person knows they have been part of a promising life-changing event. For law enforcement officers it might be an intervention at an attempted suicide, apprehension of a criminal or simply mentoring a young person. But like the iceberg, with 90 percent of its volume submerged, for most of the good any of us does we never see the results. When we listen to a child read a book or encourage her to remain drug and trouble-free, how will we ever know the degree of lasting influence we may have on that person's life? Ultimately, it doesn't matter to us. We don't need to know. You do your best. I can offer help, but I can't change the person— they must find their own empowerment—that's always their decision. With one off-duty officer it led to a resilient girl trusting a dependable adult and speaking up about the unspeakable so that she could again feel safe in her own home.

* * *

To all the kids, teachers and parents, thanks for helping me along my journey. I'm grateful that our paths have crossed. You've enriched my life.

ENDNOTES

[1] Maslow, Abraham, *The Psychology of Science* (Harper and Row, New York), 1966.

[2] Payne, Ruby, *A Framework for Understanding Poverty* (Fourth revised ed.) Highlands, TX: aha! Process, 2005), 82.

[3] Author's note: My understanding of generational poverty began and continues from exposure to the work of Dr. Ruby K. Payne. *A Framework for Understanding Poverty* helps educators work effectively with their students. *Bridges Out of Poverty: Strategies for Professionals and Communities* (Highlands, TX: aha! Process, Revised 2005) by Payne, Philip DeVol & Teri Dreussi Smith, provides a deeper understanding of people in poverty so that opportunities can be created for success.

[4] "Aerosol Irritant Projectors," (No publisher or date), 3.

[5] "Aerosol," 2.

[6] "Aerosol," 3.

[7] "Aerosol," 1.

[8] *New Testament Bible*, James 1:19-20.

[9] King Jr., Martin Luther, *Why We Can't Wait* (Harper and Row, 1963).

[10] Boy Scouts of America, *Boy Scout Handbook: A Handbook of Training for Citizenship Through Scouting.* (New Brunswick, NJ: National Council Boy Scouts of America, 1959), 19.

[11] DeLattre, Edwin J., *Character and Cops: Ethics in Policing.* (Washington, DC: American Enterprise for Public Policy Research, 1989), 31.

[12] Community Oriented Policing Services, KLETC (Kansas Law Enforcement Training Center), Regional Community Policing Training Institute at Wichita State University. U.S. Department of Justice.

[13] National Institute of Ethics, "Ethical Dilemma Test." Thanks to Dr. Neal Trautman, Ph. D. www.ethicsinstitute.com

[14] The Quotations Page, www.quotationspage.com

[15] Robbins, Anthony, Power Talk Audio Magazine: Strategies for Lifelong Success! "The Driving Force: The Six Human Needs." Vol. 26. (Robbins Research International, Inc. 1996). Author's note: How do you have a fulfilling life? I learned from Tony Robbins, leader in personal development training, how vital it is to have a passion for what you do. It makes all the difference in the world. When you really enjoy doing something and you feel like you could do it all day, every day of the week, then it must be meeting many, if not all, of the "six human needs." These needs, which drive our behavior, are certainty (comfort), uncertainty (variety), significance (importance), connection (love), growth and contribution. This vignette is a compilation of student inquiries about my job.

[16] Henderson, Randy, e-mail posted in the Reno County Sheriff's Department's back office, October 1, 2006.

[17] Boy Scouts of America, *Handbook*, 84.

[18] Potter, Jim, Ed., Reno County Sheriff's Department Newsletter, "A Day in the Life of a Typical Patrol Deputy," Good News Blues, September, 1984, V1, #7, 10-11.

[19] DeSola, Ralph, *Crime Dictionary* (New York, NY: Facts on File, Inc., 1982), 116.

[20] Potter, Jim, "DARE Outside the Classroom," Kansas Sheriff, Summer 1992, V15, #3, 19, 21.

[21] *Holy Bible—Revised Standard Version* (Thomas Nelson and Sons, New York, 1952), 674.

[22] Payne, Framework, 86. Since being exposed to Dr. Payne's work I regularly use her example in helping students understand how there are different rules for different situations.

[23] Horizons Mental Health Center, Personal Safety Awareness Program (Hutchinson, Kansas, 1983) used in curriculum developed by Richard M. Line and Susan Alexander and used in video "Better Safe Than Sorry."

[24] Gandhi, Indira, *Christian Science Monitor* (The First Church of Christ, Scientist), (Boston, Massachusetts, May 17, 1982).

[25] The Quotations Page, www.quotationspage.com

[26] Robbins, Anthony, *Awaken the Giant Within: How to Take Immediate Control of Your Mental, Emotional, Physical & Financial Destiny.* (New York: Fireside, 1992), 78-79.

[27] Family Health Administration, "What's in a Cigarette?," 1-2. (Baltimore: Maryland Department of Health & Mental Hygiene). www.fha.state.md.us

[28] Centers for Disease Control and Prevention, "Targeting Tobacco Use: The Nation's Leading Cause of Death, At a Glance 2006," (National Health Interview Surveys, 1965-2003). www.cdc.gov/tobacco

[29] U.S. Department of Health and Human Services, *Reducing Tobacco Use: A Report of the Surgeon General.* (Atlanta: U.S.

Department of Health and Human Services, Centers for Disease Control and Prevention, 2000).

[30] U.S. Department of Health and Human Services. *The Health Consequences of Involuntary Exposure to Tobacco Smoke: A Report of the Surgeon General.* (Atlanta: U.S. Department of Health and Human Services, Centers for Disease Control and Prevention, Coordinating Center for Health Promotion, National Center for Chronic Disease Prevention and Health Promotion, Office on Smoking and Health, 2006). The health effects of second-hand smoke in children is summarized at www.surgeongeneral.gov/library/secondhandsmoke/

[31] Centers for Disease Control and Prevention, "Reasons for Tobacco Use and Symptoms of Nicotine Withdrawal Among Adolescent and Young Adult Tobacco Users," (CDC, 1993). "More than 90% of young people who use tobacco daily experience at least one symptom of nicotine withdrawal (e.g., difficulty concentrating, irritability, cigarette cravings) when they have tried to quit." Tobacco Control, "Cigarette Advertising in Magazines: The Tobacco Industry Response to the Master Settlement Agreement and to Public Pressure," (Tobacco Control, 2002).

[32] National Institute on Drug Abuse, "Tobacco Addiction," (Revised July, 2006). Research Report, publication number 06-4342. www.drugabuse.gov. "Nicotine activates reward pathways—the brain circuitry that regulates the feelings of pleasure. A key brain chemical involved in mediating the desire to consume drugs is the neurotransmitter dopamine, and research has shown that nicotine increases levels of dopamine in the reward circuits...Cigarette smoking produces a rapid distribution of nicotine to the brain, with drug levels peaking within 10 seconds of inhalation. However, the acute effects of nicotine dissipate in a few minutes, as do the associated feelings of reward, which causes the smoker to continue dosing to maintain the drug's pleasurable effects and prevent withdrawal."

[33] Campaign for Tobacco-Free Kids, "Tobacco Companies Spend $28 to Market Products for Every $1 States Spend on Tobacco Prevention." (Press office release, November 30, 2005) Campaign for Tobacco-Free Kids www.tobaccofreekids.org. "In the current year, Fiscal 2006, the states combined have allocated $551 million for tobacco prevention programs, while the tobacco companies are spending an estimated $15.4 billion annually, or $42 million a day, on marketing. This means the

tobacco companies spend at least $28 to market tobacco products for every dollar the states spend on tobacco prevention. The tobacco companies spend more on marketing in a single day than 47 states and the District of Columbia spend on tobacco prevention in an entire year, the report finds."

[34] Borio, Gene, *Tobacco Timeline*, 2003. When the Revolutionary War "was over, Americans turned to tobacco taxes to help repay the revolutionary war debt." www.tobacco.org/resources/history/tobacco

[35] Campaign for Tobacco-Free Kids, "Tobacco Companies." "Tobacco use is the nation's leading preventable cause of death, killing more than 400,000 people and costing more than $180 billion in health care bills and lost productivity every year." A report, "A Broken Promise to Our Children: The 1998 State Tobacco Settlement Seven Years Later," blames "the states for not spending more on tobacco prevention programs despite collecting a record $21.3 billion this year in tobacco-generated revenue from the tobacco settlement and tobacco taxes and despite an improvement in the overall financial condition of most states after several years of tight budgets."

[36] Campaign for Tobacco-Free Kids, "Tobacco Companies," 4.

[37] Center for Disease Control and Prevention, "Targeting Tobacco Use: The Nation's Leading Cause of Death."

[38] Centers for Disease Control and Prevention, "The Percentage of U.S. Adults Who Smoke Continues to Decline—World No Tobacco Day is May 31." (Press release, May 26, 2005). www.cdc.gov/tobacco/research

[39] Campaign for Tobacco-Free Kids, "Tobacco Companies."

[40] Rigotti, MD, Nancy A., Moran, MD, MSCE, Susan E. and Wechsler, PhD, Henry, "US College Students' Exposure to Tobacco Promotions: Prevalence and Association With Tobacco Use." American Journal of Public Health, December 2004, V 94, No. 12.

[41] Essential Action, "Kicking Big Tobacco Out of Sports."

(Washington, DC: Essential Action, Global Partnerships for Tobacco Control), May, 2001. Action of the Month. www.essentialaction.org

[42] Camel Cash Catalog, www.smartsmoke.com

[43] Campaign for Tobacco-Free Kids, "Tobacco Companies," 4.

[44] World Health Organization "An International Treaty for Tobacco Control," August 12, 2003, 1. www.who.int

[45] American Association of Suicidology, "Suicide in the U.S.A.," 1. (Washington, D.C.), February, 2006. www.suicidology.org Based on 2003 statistics, "In 2003 there were 31,484 suicides in the U.S. (86 suicides per day; 1 suicide every 17 minutes). This translates to an annual suicide rate of 10.8 per 100,000." Since 1990 suicide rates in the U.S. have ranged from 10.7 to 12.4 per 100,000.

[46] Shakespeare, William, *The Merchant of Venice* (Cambridge at the University Press, 1958) edited by A.W. Verity. Act 2, Scene 2.

[47] Grossman, Dave Lt. Col., "The Bullet-Proof Mind: What It Takes to Win Violent Encounters…and After," one-day workshop at the Kansas Highway Patrol Training Center, Salina, Kansas, February 28, 2007. Author's note: My conversation was influenced by Grossman's research. I now believe that we need armed security at our schools.

[48] Potter, James K., "A Qualitative Study of School Resource Officers in Kansas." (Unpublished M.A. thesis, Lesley University, 2000), 33.

[49] Potter, "Qualitative Study," 33.

— ABOUT THE AUTHOR —

In Training

On the Job

Shelley Smith

Jim Potter has been a commissioned law enforcement officer for over twenty-five years: deputy sheriff since 1981, school resource officer (SRO) since 1988, and graduate from the National Academy at the F.B.I. Academy in Quantico, Virginia in 1990. He holds an M.A. degree in Education: "Conflict Resolution and Peaceable Schools" from Lesley University, Cambridge, Massachusetts. Potter, a former teacher, is a facilitator in youth development, strengthening families, and economic justice. He is an award-winning writer for his play "Under the Radar: Race at School." He and Alex, his wife, reside outside of Hutchinson, Kansas.

copintheclassroom.com

Order Form

Please send me ____copy/copies of *Cop in the Classroom*
at $19.95 per book (or $16.95 each for 5 or more books).
Enclosed is payment for:

Books	$ _____	
Sales Tax	$ _____	(5.3% plus any additional local sales tax for books shipped to Kansas addresses)
Subtotal	$ _____	
Shipping	$ _____	(U.S. - $4.00 first book +$2.00 each additional book)
Total	$ _____	

Ship-to Address

Name _____

Organization _____

Address _____

City _____

State_____ Zip _____

Phone _____

E-mail _____

Method of Payment

Credit card type _____ Exp _____

Credit card #_____ Vin#_____

Name on card _____

Check $ _____ Check # _____

Please make check payable to: Sandhenge Publications

copintheclassroom.com

Sandhenge Publications
P.O. Box 1172
Hutchinson, KS 67504-1172
Telephone 620-543-2539